Glorious W

Glorious Weakness

Tom Wilson

To Kathryn
with every good wish
Tom Wilson

Wide Margin

ISBN 978-0-9565943-2-7

Printed and bound in Great Britain by
Lightning Source, Milton Keynes

Glorious Weakness: A Vision of the Christian Life

Giving God glory is a strange idea, and one that provides much food for thought. At a conference I was listening to a Bible teacher describe God's glory as his essential attribute, his nature. I thoroughly agreed with her. That does appear to be the Biblical picture. The Hebrew of the Old Testament uses a word that is also translated as 'weight' or 'heaviness'; and so God's glory reminds us of his awe-inspiring nature, of how 'heavy' God is, how powerful and mighty.

And yet at the same time, the God revealed in the Old Testament is also in a sense quite vulnerable: he calls a people to himself, but they choose to ignore him, running after other gods. The prophet Hosea talks about this in his extended metaphor of his relationship with the prostitute Gomer (1:1-3, and indeed the whole book). How can a God who is described as all-powerful, as mighty, be the same one whose beloved decides a relationship with a prostitute is a better option? Of course, this choice does lead to punishment; the Exile to Babylon is an important moment in the history of Israel and one that teaches us not to take God for granted. But how exactly does it fit in with the description of a weighty, mighty, glorious God?

And turning to the New Testament, Jesus, the ultimate revelation of the glory of God, is ignored by many, despised by others, rejected and killed. How is that glorious? It certainly doesn't fit in with our normal understanding of glory or triumph. Furthermore, what exactly does it mean to give and receive glory, especially since in Revelation John has a vision of heaven in which people give God glory? In this book I want to suggest that God reveals himself in glorious weakness, and he calls us to live a life characterised by glorious weakness, a life that Jesus lived perfectly, that the Apostle Paul imitated and that we too are called to imitate.

I will begin by tracing the development of this theme throughout the Bible, before turning to the portrayal of Jesus in the Gospels, especially Luke and John. We will then look at Paul as the apostle of weakness, and at his call for cruciform imitation, urging us to imitate him as he imitates Christ. Finally we will draw the threads of our discussion together under the theme of sinning bravely as members together of the Christian family. One of my theology teachers described trying to understand the exercise of theology as 'defining the mystery' and that is what we are about to engage in. We won't get all of the details right, but we should at least have a clearer idea of this paradox of how we can be agents of God's glory through our weakness as much, if not more, than through our strength.

Tom Wilson

October 2010

Contents

Glorious Weakness throughout the Bible

The Bible is much more 'revealed reality' than it is 'revealed morality.' That is to say, Scripture isn't a list of dos and don'ts; it's not a set of rules for what to do. Rather, by reading and studying the Bible we can understand better how God sees the world, and train our eyes to see things in a similar way. So Galatians (3:15-25) speaks of the Law as a temporary teacher who trained the People of God to live in full relationship with God once Jesus came. As we read through the Bible we see the reality that God created the universe to display his glory, but that this glory is not domineering or controlling, but rather is expressed through the weakness of self-sacrificial love.

These twin themes stand in tension with each other. Without the idea of the weakness of self-sacrificial love, then glory could all too easily become domineering and overly controlling, what I'm going to call a 'triumphalist' understanding of glory. Without the idea of glory, self-sacrificial love would soon slip from weakness into complete acquiescence and a complete loss of self-identity. Held together the two ideas complement and challenge each other. There is an inherent paradox in the idea that the weakness of self-sacrificial love is in fact glorious until we understand that glory is not simply about self-promotion and betterment of the individual, but also involves mutual care and appreciation. The Trinity reveals the glory of God through mutual interdependence and unconditional self-sacrificial love.

For the purpose of this overview, we will split the story of the Bible into a six-act play, consisting of Creation; Fall; Israel; Jesus; the Church; and the End Times and New Creation. Acts 1-4 have already been fulfilled; we're in Act 5 and we know something of what Act 6 is like.

Acts 1-3 provide us with useful background, showing us how God has revealed his glorious weakness in different circumstances and situations. They also show us people trying to live out lives of glorious weakness, the People of God making all kinds of mistakes, some of which they learnt from and others of which they didn't. We can learn from their failures and disobedience, as well as their successes as we try to live similarly lives of glorious weakness.

Act 4 – Jesus – shows us how to do everything perfectly. He provides us not only with the means by which we become part of the people of God, but also with the perfect example of glorious weakness for us to imitate as we play our part in Act 5. We need to work out how Act 5 is the continuation of what has come before, and also how to fit in with what we know of what is to come. The information that we have for Act 6 is sketchy at best: perhaps best understood as general outline details of which characters are likely to do what rather than as a precise script. It's important to avoid getting too caught up in the details of Act 6 as we've deliberately been left uncertain and ignorant about all the details. God has given us the information we need. So we know Jesus will come back as judge and everyone will have to account for how they have lived their lives, we know all must submit to him on that day if not before, and we know that we don't know the precise timing.

Our focus should be on our part. We must cooperate together in Act 5: plays don't work well with single actors, but they do work when everyone plays the role assigned to them. The Christian life is one lived in community and togetherness, not in isolation: we all have our parts in the play, and in order to play our part well, we must understand what has come before as well as where the play is heading.

In the overview that follows, we will first set out a very brief understanding of each act in the play. We will then look at the two controlling metaphors of glorious weakness; the idea of the glory of God being revealed in salvation through judgement, and the idea that God manifests his character in self-sacrificial love.

Act 1: Creation: God's choice

'In the beginning God created the heavens and the earth' (Gen. 1:1).

There are a number of implications that we can draw from these opening words of the Bible. First, God existed before the world and is distinct from the world. This statement is a challenge to pantheism and animism, i.e. any religion which says that God is the same as or part of the world. God made the world out of nothing (Rom.

4:17), and so we should not worship any part of creation. To do so would be to deny God his rightful glory. In this light, remember Isaiah's sarcasm about the stupidity of idolatry (see e.g. Isa. 44).

Second, Creation itself is good. Evil is not part of the original Creation, but is Creation gone wrong. So good and evil are not equal but opposite. Good came first, from God, and is supreme; evil is a corruption of what was once good. Third, Creation is the work of the Triune God. We can form a basic Trinitarian understanding of creation in this way: God the Father is the source of everything that exists, the one who speaks his Word in creation (Gen. 1-3; Psalm 33). God the Son is the Word spoken in Creation (see John 1:1-18). Creation comes about through Jesus (see Prov. 8; Col. 1; Heb. 1:3). God the Holy Spirit is the power through whom creation takes place (Gen. 1, Rom. 8). Finally, we know that God cares for what he has made, and will complete his purpose for it (Rom. 8:18-21). One helpful way of understanding God's involvement in the world is the picture used by the early church teacher Irenaeus, who described the Son and the Spirit as the two hands of God the Father, the means by which he touches, shapes and influences all creation.

All this means that the act of creation displays the glory of God; creation itself witnesses to who God is and how he is sovereign over all (Psalm 8; Rom. 1:20). When everything is made it is perfect (Gen. 1:31), and so in no need of God's saving action. Furthermore, the New Testament states that the world, which we can take to include human beings, was made to glorify Jesus (see Rom. 8:19-21; Phil. 2:11).

Creation is also the manifestation of God's love. God did not need to create, he choose to create. Thus Creation is contingent on God, not the other way around. Since God created the world knowing that God the Son would have to suffer and die to redeem it (1 Pet. 1:20; see also Rev. 13:8), the act of creation is itself an act of self-sacrificial love. The fact that God made us free to choose to love him or to reject him is also an important reminder of God's love; our free choice is a sign of God's glorious weakness, wanting genuine love that is freely chosen rather than forced obedience. Through the act of creation, we are also assured of how much God loves us and the world he has made (John 3:16 etc).

Act 2: Fall: Human rebellion

Once, when listening to a radio interview of a clergyman on BBC Radio 4's Today program, I heard the interviewer suggest that it was discriminatory to say that a particular action was sinful. I can't remember what the clergyman said in reply, but I know what my answer would have been. Describing someone as sinful is in no way discriminatory, because everyone is guilty of sinning. The sinful nature is just as universal as death – everyone is a sinner and everyone will die. Sin can be seen in the world, but you need God's eyes to see it, since as Paul puts it: 'The god of this age has blinded the minds of unbelievers, so that they cannot see the light of the gospel of the glory of Christ, who is the image of God' (2 Cor. 4:4).

Sin should not be defined primarily in terms of action, but in terms of attitude and relationship. As Peter Lewis states:

> 'Sin is not properly understood until it is seen in terms of our relationship with God our creator and his acknowledged and welcomed Lordship in our lives. A life of sin is not necessarily a scandalous life; it might be a very respected, useful and admired life. But if it is God-less it is profoundly sinful. Sin is a flight from, a rebellion against, and an antipathy to God, where self is central and supreme. Sin is not simply a broken code but a broken relationship; not only a relationship lost but a relationship renounced.'[1]

Although the idea of sin may be an uncomfortable one, it is one we cannot escape from if we accept the Bible's understanding of human nature. Sin impacts every area of our lives ('The heart is deceitful above all things and beyond cure. Who can understand it?' Jer. 17:9). The most basic sin is idolatry, which we can define as worship of something other than God. A sinful life is thus one that puts self at the centre and says no to an offer of love (a point made repeatedly by the Old Testament prophets, e.g. Ezek. 16).

The self-sacrificial love of God is emphasised in the fact that God created human beings knowing that they would reject him and try to run their own lives, and in the process ruin them. Only a loving God would not have completely destroyed humanity at this point. The Fall means that the image of God in us is spoilt, although the damage is not

1 Lewis, *The Message of the Living God*, page 72.

irrevocable. Our rebellion against God deserves death, but we do not get what we deserve. Rather God chooses to display his glory in salvation through judgement. Sin is serious and its consequences cannot be escaped, but the self-sacrificial love of God means that Jesus is the one who suffers the judgement so that we can experience salvation. There is even a hint of this at the very moment of the Fall (see Gen. 3:15).

Act 3: Israel: God calls a People to Himself

This is the most involved act of the play: getting all the characters in the right place can be difficult! The aim of this chapter is to give an overview, not spend too long on any one character, and so we will simply note the outline of Israel's history. I have divided the life of the People of God into ten stages:

• Calling of the people of God, the days of the Patriarchs;

• Time in Egypt, leading to the Exodus;

• Wilderness wanderings;

• Entry into the Land and the initial conquest;

• The period of the Judges;

• The united monarchy under Saul, David and Solomon;

• The subsequent divided monarchy and the time of two kingdoms;

- The exile to Babylon;

- Restoration of the people to the land;

- Waiting and hoping for a Messiah.

The theme of glorious weakness runs right through the story of Israel. God continually displays his love for his people. Time and again, they reject him, choosing to serve their own interests rather than be obedient to him. They regularly rebel, preferring allegiance to other gods to loyalty to Yahweh. The prophets often speak of the sin of idolatry in terms of adultery, making it clear just how much the actions of the people of Israel are a rejection of an offer of love. God's love is a very costly and pain-filled love. This is spelt out in detail by Hosea's painful experience of marrying a prostitute who is repeatedly unfaithful to him; God tells him this is exactly how the people of Israel have treated their God.

We must also be aware that God chooses the people of Israel not for their own sake, but in order to display his glory to the nations (e.g. God's statement that he made the whole house of Judah that 'they might be for me a people, a name, a praise and a glory' Jer. 13:11). Israel's rebellion does not go unpunished; God's love is not spineless. It is long-suffering, but there are limits, and once they are reached, then judgment follows. There are numerous warnings, but since they are ignored, judgement is enacted. But it is not final; prophecies of judgement are normally followed by messages of hope. God always keeps a remnant for himself. It is through them that his glory and his mercy are displayed to the world. A clear example of this is seen in Ezekiel 16. It tells of how Israel failed to respond to the offer of love from Yahweh, preferring prostitution with the surrounding nations. This unfaithfulness is punished; but at the end of the chapter there is still a message of hope and restoration.

The Glory of Yahweh

The phrase 'the glory of Yahweh' occurs in many places in the Old Testament, almost always in connection with salvation and judgement. If we think back over the ten stages in the life of the people of God that we identified above we can see how the glory of God appears during each of them. The Patriarchs have regular experiences of the glory of God, perhaps most notably during the covenant ceremony for Abraham (Gen. 15:12, 17) and Jacob wrestling with God (Gen. 32:22-32). This second experience is an interesting display of glorious weakness, as God does not beat Jacob soundly but wrestles with him in order to change him. While the people are in Egypt, Moses receives a revelation of God's glory through God's appearance in the burning bush, and again God is gentle but firm with Moses, who does as he is commanded, but is able to express his fears and doubts (Exod. 3, 6).

God's glory is seen a number of times during the period in the desert, including Exodus 16:7, 10, where the glory of Yahweh appears in response to the grumbling of the people, condemning their lack of faith and providing for their needs. In Exodus 24:16, 17 the glory of Yahweh appears on Mount Sinai when Moses goes up the mountain to meet God. The covenant made there provides access to the saving presence of God, but the regulations Moses receives are in themselves a judgement because without them God cannot be approached. When the judgement of God falls on the sacrifice for the consecration of Aaron and his sons in Leviticus 9:6, the glory of Yahweh appears in 9:23. As God pardons the people through Moses' intercession after their rebellion in response to the bad report of the spies (Num. 14:20), Yahweh assures the people that the earth will be filled with his glory in Numbers 14:21.

During the conquest and the time of the judges, God's glorious weakness is seen in how he deals with the people: they are not forced to trust him and worship him, but rather must choose to do so, and they often don't make this choice, invariably with disastrous results. Moving forward to the time of the united monarchy, the glory of Yahweh becomes manifest when sacrifices are made for the dedication of the temple (1 Kings 8:11; 2 Chr. 5:14; 7:2).

Throughout the time of the divided monarchy and the exile, the prophets regularly speak of God's glory. Taking just a few examples, Isaiah 34 presents apocalyptic judgements, and these are followed by the promise that the redeemed shall see the glory of Yahweh (Isa. 35:2). The manifestation of Yahweh's glory in Isaiah 40:5 is similar in that it follows the double payment for sin in 40:2. Likewise Isaiah 58:8 promises the protection of Yahweh's glory after unrighteous piety is denounced in 58:3-5. Ezekiel receives a vision of the glory of Yahweh (Ezek. 1:28; 3:12, 23), as the nation suffers the judgement of exile. He sees the glory of Yahweh depart in judgement (Ezek. 10:4, 18; 11:23), only to return in restoration (43:5; 44:4).

The theme of God's glory is not limited to the occurrences of the phrase 'the glory of Yahweh.'[2] Noah and his family are saved through the waters of judgement. The children of Israel are delivered from slavery through God's judgement on Egypt. The redeemed will praise God for his mercy as they see his righteous judgement. God's renown is the song of the remnant throughout salvation history (e.g. Isa. 26:8), and the New Testament suggests this will be their song in the ages to come (Rev. 7:9-12). This way of approaching the topic broadens the discussion out from a mere word study of the occurrences of 'glory'. Even where those words are not used, the texts point to the reputation that God gains for himself (Josh. 2:9-13) as he reveals his justice that he might make known the meaning of his mercy (Rom. 9:22-23).

The idea of God's glory is also reflected in God's concern for his name, which reveals his character, manifesting his glory. This can be seen in Exodus 33:18-19:

> Then Moses said, "Now show me your glory." And the LORD said, "I will cause all my goodness to pass in front of you, and I will proclaim my name, the LORD, in your presence. I will have mercy on whom I will have mercy, and I will have compassion on whom I will have compassion.

By proclaiming his own sovereign freedom in his name, God is revealing his glory to Moses.

---

2 What follows in this section is based on Hamilton, 'The Glory of God in Salvation Through Judgement: The Centre of Biblical Theology?'.

God intends to be known, thus the common refrain, 'And you shall know that I am Yahweh.' This self-revelatory statement is peppered throughout the Old Testament, but Yahweh is presented as making this assertion ten times in Exodus, and he insists on it another sixty-eight times in Ezekiel.[3] Jeremiah also makes it clear that God calls a people to himself for his glory (Jer. 13:11. See also Isa. 43:7; 66:18; Jer. 33:9).

Although God's glory is clearly revealed in this way, and it is overwhelming to those who see it, it is nevertheless not as all consuming as we might think. God is concerned for his glory, but he is also concerned for his people; he still loves them and cares for them. The dialogue in Malachi is a good example of this 'weaker' manifestation of God's glory as the doubts and failures of the people are brought into the open and discussed. Overall we see the glorious weakness of a God whose mercy triumphs over judgement, who right from the beginning calls people to related to

3 For texts that declare that people or other things *will know that I am Yahweh* (and related expressions), see Exod. 6:7; 7:5, 17; 8:22; 10:2; 14:4, 18; 16:12; 29:46; 31:13; Deut. 29:5; 1 Kgs 20:13, 28; Isa. 45:3; 49:23, 26; 60:16; Jer. 9:24; 24:7; Ezek. 5:13; 6:7, 10, 13, 14; 7:4, 9, 27; 11:10, 12; 12:15, 16, 20; 13:14, 21, 23; 14:8; 15:7; 16:62; 17:21, 24; 20:12, 20, 38, 42, 44; 21:4, 5; 22:16, 22; 24:27; 25:5, 7, 11, 17; 26:6, 14; 28:22, 23, 26; 29:6, 9, 21; 30:8, 19, 25, 26; 32:15; 33:29; 34:27, 30; 35:4, 9, 12, 15; 36:11, 23, 36, 38; 37:6, 13, 14, 28; 38:23; 39:6, 7, 22, 28; Joel 3:17. At several points God is presented as acting on behalf of his name (1 Sam. 12:22; Isa. 48:9; Ezek. 20:9, 14, 22, 44), and he acts for his own sake (cf. 2 Kgs 19:34; 20:6; Isa. 37:35; 43:25; 48:11). God emphasizes his own uniqueness asking, 'Who is like me?' (Isa. 44:7; Jer. 49:19; 50:44; cf. Isa. 46:5), and declaring 'there is none besides me' (Isa. 45:6, 21; cf. 46:9).

him in spite of their weakness and failure, who uses the most unlikely people as his chosen agents. There is much more that could be said to expand on this theme, but we will move on to the glorious weakness that is shown perfectly in the life of Jesus.

Act 4: Jesus: God with us

The events of Jesus' life are quite well known. Here we are only looking at the basic chronology (the order of what happens when). We can see the theme of glorious weakness running through the whole of Jesus' life; I'll make a few brief comments here, and we'll unpack the idea in much more detail in the next chapter.

1. Birth: the eternal becomes involved in time

Jesus, begotten from God the Father from all eternity, has his human birth from his mother Mary at a particular instant in history. So whilst the Father and the Holy Spirit are both involved in history, only the Son *becomes* history. This affirms our humanity; reminding us that God thinks flesh and blood are good things to be celebrated and enjoyed. The fact that God the Son took on human likeness, and was born of a virgin in circumstances open to misinterpretation, is a clear sign of God's glorious weakness. Jesus' obscure origins mean he is in danger of rejection, but he chooses to make his glory known in this way so only those who truly love him enter into relationship with him.

2. Growth in holiness

We know virtually nothing of Jesus' early life, apart from a few snippets in Luke 2. This lack of heritage is a further sign of glorious weakness, as in the first century lineage and ancestry were important for establishing a person's status.

3. Baptism

Jesus' identity and mission as the Son of God are affirmed. He shows glorious weakness in identifying with sinful humanity.

4. Temptation

Jesus goes into the wilderness to prepare himself and to make his own calling and motivation sure.

5. Public ministry

> 'The time has come,' Jesus said. 'The kingdom of God is near. Repent and believe the good news!' (Mark 1:15)

Jesus travels around both teaching and healing, acting for the mind and for the body, demonstrating a holistic ministry to the whole person. Jesus calls and trains his followers: the disciples spend time with Jesus, learning from his teaching and watching him in action. They are also sent out in pairs on missionary journeys, learning at first hand how to proclaim the kingdom of God. It was all to one purpose: Jesus was a man born to die, and so when the time came he set out to Jerusalem. Jesus knows he will die, and warns his followers about this. They don't quite understand it all. See Matthew 16:21-28; 20:17-19; Luke 9:22; 18:31-34. The miracles and Jesus' death are ultimately displays of God's glory, but the disciples' failure to understand is a sign of his weakness.

6. The events of that final week

These events are in no way triumphalist; and so are misunderstood by many. But for those with the eyes to see, they display the true glory of God.

Triumphal Entry: coming to Jerusalem as king, in weakness and humility, riding on a donkey.

Cleansing the Temple: showing the lack of true relationship with God in Israel: there was much outward show, but little heart to heart relationship. God's weakness in allowing others to reject him is made clear.

The Last Supper: preparing the disciples for his death, and giving them a meal to remember him by. Jesus shows the extent of his self-sacrificial love by washing his disciples' feet and by instituting the Last Supper.

Gethsemane: the final moment of choice, when Jesus decides to obey not his own will, but the Father's. His glorious weakness and humility are shown in his willingness to stay and face a painful death rather than escape to freedom.

Glorious Weakness

The Trials: under both the Jewish and the Roman authorities, where Jesus refuses to engage in a power struggle, and weakly submits to the miscarriage of justice.

Death: the agony of crucifixion, dying to fulfil the Scriptures, as God's glory is shown in the world.

Resurrection: proving that Jesus' claims were accurate, and displaying God's glorious power to all the world.

7. Ascension

Jesus' resurrection appearances make it clear that he has defeated death and passed through to new, resurrection life. Having shown God's glory in its fullness to his followers, Jesus then returns to his Father. As a result of all this, Jesus sent his disciples out into the world: not on their own, but in the power of the Holy Spirit, and so the Church begins to grow.

Jesus shows us glorious weakness

Jesus, God in human flesh, is the supreme demonstration of the self-sacrificial love of God. He chooses to die for us of his own free will, and what is more chooses to do so while we are still enemies of God, in open rebellion against him (Romans 5:5-8). Jesus demonstrates the nature of his self-sacrificial love through a simple act of humble service, washing his disciples' feet (John 13:1-17), before reminding them that death for others is the supreme demonstration of love (John 15:13), a death he then willingly embraces.

Jesus is the perfect manifestation of God's glory, who is both fully God and fully human. But what exactly is the glory of God as manifest in Jesus? It is not what we might initially expect – it is not overbearing or dominant, but rather filled with humility and self-sacrifice – we see this in a number of places in the Gospel accounts, which we will explore more fully in the next chapter.

Act 5: The Church: God sends us!

As the Church, God's people in the world, we are called to live out the Great Commission:

> Then Jesus came to them and said, "All authority in heaven and on earth has been given to me. Therefore go and make disciples of all nations, baptising them in the name of the Father and of the Son and of the Holy Spirit, and teaching them to obey everything I have commanded you. And surely I am with you always, to the very end of the age." (Matt. 28:18-20)

The book of Acts only gives us a bit of the story, and the letters give us a few more hints, but the picture is by no means complete. We can also learn from studying the history of other periods of the church: it forms a helpful complement. It does not have the authority of Scripture, but still has much to teach us. If nothing else it should help us to avoid making the same mistakes! Church tradition and history can be thought of as second order stories, giving us hints as to how to continue this act. The more you read about the church, the more you can see the theme of glorious weakness running as a thread through all the ages and generations.

What is the church?

There are many elements to an understanding of what the church is, but the most important one is that the church is a group of people, and not a building. Two possible definitions are (1) that the church is the counter-cultural community of discipleship that God calls to challenge the world, or (2) the church is the community of the pilgrim people of God influenced and directed by the Bible, equipped and empowered by the Holy Spirit, fully living in the present whilst also being focused on the future and life with Jesus for all eternity.

The book of Acts gives us some hints as to how the church is to function in the world. The progression of the Gospel from Jerusalem and Judea, to Samaria, and from there to the ends of the earth suggests that we should begin by relating the gospel to those closest to us, and then gradually move further and further a field. Paul's missionary journeys, both his work in pioneer church planting and also in visiting and strengthening existing churches can also act as inspiration for us.

The church should be characterised by the same self-sacrificial love that Jesus displayed to the world, and when it is at its best, it does indeed manage that. This love should be shown both to the community of the church and also to those who remain outside. Our fallen, sinful nature means there will always be some differences in how this love is shown, but we should strive to love everyone equally.

Equally, the church is the vehicle God uses to display his glory to the world, a glory that comes in our individual and corporate salvation through the judgement that fell on Jesus. We therefore show what it means to be saved and display God's glory in this act of salvation. The body of Christ, equipped and empowered by God's Spirit, are called to reveal the Father's glory to the world. We do this both in and through our individual acts of faith, and also through our corporate life together.

It is important to note that both self-sacrificial love and displaying God's glory are more corporate than individual. Self-sacrificial love must, by definition, involve groups of people, and we are saved to form a community that displays God's glory to the world, not as individuals who then remain in isolation. This more collective understanding of what it means to be church is an important corrective to an increasingly individualised Western Christianity.

As a church we are called to live in such a way that we make God's glory known to the whole world. In discussing Christian freedom in regard to what we eat, Paul suggests that 'whether you eat or drink or whatever you do, do it all for the glory of God' (1 Cor. 10:31). This is how the church is called to live. We will look at Paul's glorious weakness and his call to imitate Christ in more detail in later chapters, but first we will press on to the home straight and look at our final act.

Act 6: The End Times: God makes everything perfect

The details of exactly what will happen at the end of time are sketchy and disputed. We will do our best to avoid getting caught up in speculation over the details. First, we must remember that the timing is unknown (Mark 13 etc), and so we cannot decide for ourselves when the world will end. All those who have tried have ended up looking very foolish.

But whilst it is the case that the timing is unknown, the central reality of what will happen is clear. There will be a judgement: everyone will have to give an account of how they have lived. Our actions now have eternal consequences: We only have one chance to take up our role in the play, but the impact is eternal. We will be raised physically from the dead, and all creation will be restored and made perfect; the new heaven and new earth are not just a spiritual dream world.

Knowing how the play ends will impact how we play our part in the middle of the play. There are thus two main reasons why we know what we do know. The first concerns motivation (Phil. 1:21; Heb. 9:22 etc). Knowing there will be a judgement and that we will have to give an account of our lives should be an important factor in motivating our present behaviour. This is related to the second reason, that of preparation. Matthew 25 is key for understanding this. In particular the parable of the sheep and the goats (25:31-46) reminds us that Christianity must be practised to be real. The same point is made by James (1:22-25; 2:14-26).

But that doesn't mean we need to know all the details. Jesus implies that full knowledge is unnecessary (Mark 13). Indeed, it would be demotivating. If we knew when we would die, we would act differently. The best tests are those you don't know are tests; a surprise inspection is the one that reveals the real state of affairs. Ultimately such revelation is all in the hands of God: it is his choice, not ours!

Once creation is made perfect and we have all passed through judgement to reach salvation and have our prefect resurrection bodies, then the glory of God will be displayed for all to see, and we will all enjoy celebrating God's presence with us. The sacrifice of love will also be complete, and everyone will be able to love each other perfectly with no fear of hurt or pain.

James Hamilton suggests:

> For examples of the vindicated offering praise and glory to God immediately following his judgement, see the opening of the seals in Rev. 6:1-14, followed by the description of the 144,000 sealed (who will apparently be saved: 7:3) in 7:1-8, and it seems that the praises in 7:9-12 are in response to the salvation (7:10) which comes through judgement. Cf. also the judgement of 11:13-14, followed by the praise of 11:15-19; judgement in 12:7-9, followed by the praises of the saved in 12:10-12; the introduction of the culmination of God's wrath in 15:1 is followed by praise to God's glory in 15:2-4; spliced into the account of the outpouring of the wrath

of God in the bowls in 16:1-21 is the praise of God's justice in 16:5-7; as the friends of Babylon mourn her judgement in 18:19, the vindicated are called to rejoice in 18:20; once judgement is finally completed in 20:11-15, the new heavens and the new earth radiate with God's glory (21:23; 22:5) in chs. 21-22. The closing chapters of the Apocalypse are punctuated by the command, 'Worship God' (19:10; 22:9).[4]

Thus the Scriptures close with a clear command to give God the glory he deserves.

Conclusion

From creation to new creation, God's glorious weakness runs through his dealing with his people. God's glory is not triumphalist or controlling, forcing people to worship. Rather it is displayed in self-sacrifical love, and nowhere more so that in the person and work of Jesus.

4   Hamilton, 'The Glory of God in Salvation Through Judgement: The Centre of Biblical Theology?'. The quote is from page 79, footnote 86.

Glorious Weakness in the Life of Jesus

Jesus lived in an era that took glory seriously. The cult of the Roman emperor placed a high value on his status and significance in the world, which meant that when people in the first century heard about glory, the first thing that would come to mind would have been emperor worship. Scholars debate how compulsory emperor worship was; it is likely that the degree of coercion was quite variable, both across the empire and also depending on which emperor was in power. But however strongly the cult was pushed, there was an expectation that the emperor was someone to be glorified. The glory of the emperor was triumphalist and dominant, impacting all society. By contrast we will see the life of Jesus was one of glorious weakness.

The Glory of the Emperor and the Gods

The emperor cult was an inescapable fact of life: anyone who wished to take part in society would encounter it at some point.[5] Festivals were held on the emperor's birthday and days commemorating his achievements. The benefactors of the imperial cult sponsored all public entertainments, such as gladiatorial fights, athletics

---

5 What follows is based on Barr, 'John's Ironic Empire'.

contests and music performances. It was a source of civic pride for a city to have an imperial temple, and a great personal achievement to be a priest there. This meant it was an honour given only to the most important people. All forms of civic engagement involved gods, and making sacrifices to them was an important start to any meeting or civic function. At home and among any private associations there were also gods to be invoked. Such religious ceremonies were integral to normal life, and giving glory to gods and to the emperor a routine fact of daily interaction.

The emperor was thought of as 'lord of all,' both the living and the dead, and so when Christians used that, or similar, phrases to describe Jesus, they were effectively engaged in a direct challenge to the authority of the emperor, and in a competition for who should be glorified.[6] Paul regularly describes Jesus as having complete authority, at least in part as a challenge to the emperor. For example he says Jesus is Lord of both the living and the dead (Rom. 14:9); that he will judge both living and the dead (2 Tim. 4:1); and that whether we live or die, we belong to Jesus (1 Thess. 5:10).

An Alternative Empire

The Gospel writers are equally clear that it is Jesus, not the emperor, who is worthy of receiving glory and honour. Warren Carter is clear that Matthew is written

---

6   What follows is based on Howell, 'The imperial authority and benefaction of centurions of Acts 10.34-43: a response to C. Kavin Rowe'.

from an anti-imperial stance, establishing God's empire as a challenge to the Roman empire:[7]

> 'Matthew's plot is an act of imperial negotiation. Unfolding through six stages, its central dynamic comprises conflict between Jesus and the Rome-allied (Jerusalem based) leaders. It ends with God raising Jesus, crucified by the imperial elite.'

The order is:

1:1-4:16 God initiates the story in the conception and commissioning of Jesus to manifest God's saving presence. Jesus is threatened by Herod, witnessed to by John, sanctioned by God in baptism, tempted by the devil, and validated by Scripture. The alternative empire is introduced and the competing claims for allegiance are set out.

4:17-11:1 Jesus manifests God's saving presence, the kingdom or empire of God, through constituting a community of followers, preaching, healing, and exorcizing. The character of God's alternative empire is made clear and the invitation to join it is given out.

11:2-16:20 Jesus' actions and words continue to reveal his identity as God's agent and the life giving purposes of God's empire. He draws positive and negative responses as some choose to join his empire and others prefer the status quo. Powerful elites end up in conflict with him over his societal vision and practices.

---

7   Carter, 'Matthew's Gospel: An Anti-Imperial/Imperial Reading'. The quote is from page 424.

Glorious Weakness

16:21-20:34 Jesus teaches his followers that conflict with the elite will result in his crucifixion in Jerusalem and God's resurrection of him from the dead. This event has numerous implications for their lives as followers. The true nature of the glorious weakness of the alternative empire is made clear.

21:1-27:66 Jesus enters Jerusalem, challenges the centre of the elite's power in the temple, conflicts with them over societal leadership, and condemns their world as temporary and facing imminent destruction under God's judgment. The alliance of Jerusalem leaders and the Roman governor crucifies him. Conflict between the two empires was inevitable and has now come about. It looks as if the empire of this world has won, and God's alternative empire has been defeated. But the story is not over yet.

28:1-20 God's saving purposes overcome the worst that the elite can do and expose the limits of imperial power by raising Jesus. Jesus participates in God's authority over all creation. He commissions his followers to worldwide mission, promising to be with them. The alternative empire triumphs and God's glorious weakness is vindicated.

Similarly, Mark's gospel understands Jesus as the one who has absolute authority and power. He is not to be taken lightly, but must be obeyed completely. Jesus' first public words in Mark are an announcement of the arrival of the kingdom of God (1:15), and from that point on, Jesus sets himself on a collision course with all other sources of authority, be they Jewish, Roman or spiritual/demonic. We have seen the stages of how the alternative empire is revealed in Matthew and we will take a more detailed look at the glorious weakness of Jesus in Luke and John. But Mark has his own distinct points to make.

The glorious weakness of Jesus' ministry is seen in the parable of the sower (Mark 4:1-20). Here is a farmer who really has no idea of how to work the land: he wastes vast amounts of his seed by scattering it on the path, amongst thorns and weeds and on poor soil. But that does not matter, for the farmer wants to give every area a chance to produce a crop, even though many will fail to do so. In the same way, Jesus chooses the glorious weakness of giving everyone the chance to respond to his message, regardless of the fact that many will chose to reject him. Jesus chooses the way of the cross, a path of self-denial, of embracing rejection and suffering for the sake of the redemption of many. This understanding is outline first in 8:34-38, and then spelt out more fully in 9:30-37, where Jesus commends the humility and weakness of a child as a model for discipleship. The theme receives its fullest expression in Mark in Jesus' third prediction of his death (10:32-45), where he says clearly that he will suffer rejection, beating and death. James and John respond by asking for places of power and authority in Jesus' kingdom. Jesus is clear that those places are not his to grant; instead of seeking such exaltation he commends the way of glorious weakness, telling his followers

> 'whoever wants to become great among you must be your servant, and whoever wants to be first must be slave of all. For even the Son of Man did not come to be served, but to serve, and to give his life as a ransom for many' (10:43-45).

Glorious Weakness

This is Mark's most succinct expression of the idea of glorious weakness, that the way to achieve glory is to be humble, weak, a servant of all and master of none, one who is prepared to give up everything for the sake of God and his kingdom. Only those who freely choose to do this will ultimately be vindicated and become the means by which God displays his glory to the world, as God's kingdom triumphs over the triumphalism of the world.

Luke and John also have this understanding of the dominance of the kingdom of God over against other sources of authority. What we must recognise is that not only do they have a different power base, but the understanding of power and glory is also very different. We will look in more detail at how the alternative empire is portrayed in Luke and in John.

Luke's understanding of Jesus' glory[8]

Thomas Martin suggests that in Luke's Gospel, Jesus' glory is primarily his humility. He comments that in Luke there is a tension between 'glory' and 'humility'. And he also notes that sometimes 'glory' is understood in the sense of 'triumphalism', the notion of control and dominance. But he says that when 'glory' is used in reference to Jesus, it is always linked with humility and signals an inversion of our normal understanding; it is a counter-sign of our normal expectations of kings, princes, rulers, presidents, splendidly robed bishops, well-dressed church leaders,

---

8   What follows is based largely on Martin, 'What Makes Glory Glorious?'.

those who have much while the ordinary people have little or nothing.[9]

Jesus' glory, then, is found primarily not in triumph or in splendour, but in weakness and in humility. Martin talks about 'kenosis', the idea of self-emptying in service of others. It is an idea most succinctly expressed in Paul's comment in Philippians that Jesus did not consider equality with God something to be grasped, but made himself nothing, taking on the very nature of a servant, being made in human likeness (2:7). The idea is thus that when the gospels portray Jesus' glory and his empire, they do not understand these things as something splendid or magnificent, but rather as something weak and humble. It is true that Jesus is Lord of all creation, but he displays that lordship through glorious weakness, not through dominance and control.

This theme runs right throughout Luke's gospel. Jesus' virgin birth is true display of glorious weakness. Few would have believed Mary's story of the angel Gabriel visiting her; many would have thought she was lying, and had engaged in sex outside of marriage. Jesus chooses the weakness and humility of this birth rather than a triumphalist appearance that would force people to worship him (1:26-38). Jesus is born in humility, placed in a manger, his family unable to stay in a guest room (2:7). The only visitors Luke records are the shepherds, societal outcasts that no one really wanted to associate with (2:8-20). Jesus' first public action is one of humility: he comes to John to receive the baptism of repentance, even though he himself has no need of it, in order to further identify

9   Martin, 'What Makes Glory Glorious?', page 5, footnote 7.

himself with those he came to save (3:21-22). When faced with temptation in the desert, he does not overcome Satan with a mighty display of power and authority, but through humble reliance of prayer and the word of God (4:1-13).

Jesus then returns to his own hometown of Nazareth. His public teaching ministry has started, and people are praising his teaching authority (4:14-15), yet when he declares this in Nazareth, their response is unbelief and an attempt to throw him off a cliff in order to stone him for blasphemy. This does not end in tragedy, as Jesus is able to simply walk through the crowd. He does not force them to believe through a display of power, but simply displays his humility, leaving them in their unbelief (4:16-30).

Jesus' ministry is a powerful one: he has great teaching authority, performs many spectacular miracles and calls many to follow him. But even when he chooses his twelve closest followers we see a further sign of his glorious weakness, as he deliberately chooses someone who would ultimately betray him (6:16). The sermon on the plain (6:20-26) is a further display of glory in weakness, as blessing is spoken on the poor, the hungry, those who weep and are persecuted for their faith. Woes are spoken on those who might ordinarily be considered glorious: the rich, the well fed, the happy, those who are continually praised and well spoken of. There is a challenge to our normal value systems: what we consider glorious is in fact valueless, and what we consider weak is actually a true display of glory.

This point is clearly made in Jesus' next teaching, about love for our enemies (6:27-36). Treating well those who treat you well is simply normal daily living: the children of the kingdom are to love those who do not love them. They display God's glory through their weakness in returning evil with good, hatred with love, distain with compassion. Often we may struggle to think of people we could describe as our enemies, but we all have people who irritate us, annoy us and generally get on our nerves. And Jesus is teaching us here to pray for those people just as much as for an enemy who might try to attack us. The point of such prayers is as much to give us the opportunity to become more like Jesus and display God's glorious weakness to the world, as it is to change the person who is prayed for. The same could be said concerning the instructions regarding judging (6:37-43): we are to ensure our own standing is right before God before we look to challenge anyone else.

Jesus' glorious weakness is also seen in those he regularly associates with. Amongst all four gospels, Luke in particular wants us to notice how Jesus crosses societal boundaries and challenges taboos. Jewish society in the first century was strongly patriarchal and looked down on foreigners and anyone who was ill or otherwise unclean. And yet these are the very people that Jesus spends the most time with, and praises at the expense of those who might normally be considered powerful and worthy of glory (i.e. Jewish men).

Thus the centurion who comes to Jesus asking for his servant to be healed is praised as having faith greater than that found in Israel, simply because he takes Jesus at his word, and does not demand he comes to his house to perform the healing miracle (7:1-10). Jesus raises the widow's son, because he is concerned for her welfare and the suffering she will face as a sonless widow (7:11-17). He heals the demon possessed (8:26-39); is happy to heal the woman who has been bleeding for twelve years, ensuring the healing is made public so she can reintegrate into society (8:43-48), and raises a dead girl to life (8:49-56). Jesus wants to eat with Zacchaeus, an outcast because he is a tax collector and so linked with the occupying Roman authorities (19:1-10). These are all people on the margins of society, and Jesus chooses them as his companions, demonstrating he is not interested in triumphalism or human authority, but in humble service and care for those who are broken. A further sign of Jesus' glorious weakness is seen in how badly his actions are misunderstood, as he is accused of being a glutton and a drunkard (7:34) and of performing miracles by the power of Beelzebul, the prince of demons (11:14-20).

The fact that Jesus is prepared to be served is a further demonstration of his glorious weakness. This is shown most clearly in Luke in the incident where Jesus is anointed by a 'sinful woman' (7:36-50). Jesus is eating at a Pharisee's house, and a woman 'who had lived a sinful life' (7:37) comes in and wets his feet with her tears, wipes them with her hair, kissed them and poured perfume on them. Perhaps she originally intended to anoint Jesus' head, but her emotions got the better of her. Whatever her intentions, her actions are highly provocative, to say the least. Joel Green notes that in her cultural context, where women were readily viewed as sex objects, her behaviour would have been regarded by the men present as quite erotic: letting her hair down was on a par with appearing topless, and she would have appeared to be fondling Jesus' feet, like a prostitute used to providing sexual favours.[10] And Jesus not only lets her do this, but even commends her actions, despite all the problematic misinterpretations that result. He is glorified by her worship and her love, even though it could be – and was – seriously misunderstood. There is glory, then, in the weakness of accepting faulty and faltering praise and love, rather than in elaborate phrasing and carefully choreographed ritual.

Jesus' transfiguration (9:28-36) might most naturally be taken as an example of triumphalist glory. It is certainly true that the disciples see the full extent of Jesus' glory: the change in his face, and his clothes as bright as a flash of lightning. They see him talking with Moses and Elijah, representing the Law and the Prophets, the great history of the people of God (9:29-30). Yet, as Martin notes, it is only later, in the dark cloud, that God speaks and commends his Son as the chosen one whom they must listen to (9:35).[11] The suggestion is therefore that it is this harder-to-notice Jesus, the Jesus who is alone, whose glory is hidden in his weakness, who is the one the Father commends us to follow.

This is certainly what is commended to the disciples in the section which follows. Jesus comes down the mountain, back to the problems of a broken world: the disciples are unable to heal the demon-possessed boy, and so Jesus has to do it for them (9:37-43). Jesus reminds his disciples of his glorious weakness, of how he must die in order for them to live, but they do not understand him

10   Green, *New International Commentary on the New Testament: The Gospel of Luke*, page 310.
11   Martin, 'What Makes Glory Glorious?', page 22.

(9:43-45). The irony of the misunderstanding is made plain by the argument that follows: the disciples argue over who is the greatest, arguing in effect over who deserves the most glory. And so Jesus gives them a visual reminder of glorious weakness, bringing a child into their midst and telling them to welcome children as a means of welcoming him and his Father (9:46-48).

This saying about welcoming children has caused much confusion over the years, but the focus of our study should help make the point clear. Children in Jesus' day were powerless, at a young age not even really regarded as human beings, a group completely lacking in triumphalist glory. And these are the people Jesus wants his disciples to welcome and be like: those whose glory is seen in their weakness and their dependence on others – ultimately on the Father – for all things, for life and for salvation. Glorious weakness is shown in humility and trust and reliance on others.

The final point in Luke's gospel that we will touch on is the triumphal entry: Jesus enters Jerusalem as a king, but not as a violent warrior king, on a proud warhorse, triumphant in victory. That kind of triumph was the province of the Roman emperors: thousands upon thousands would line the streets of Rome to welcome a victorious emperor. The whole process fed the ego so much that a slave stood behind the emperor in his chariot and would whisper periodically in his ear 'remember you are but a man' – a clear sign that a Roman triumph was designed to make the emperor think he was a god.

There is no danger of such confusion occurring for Jesus' triumphal entry (19:28-40). The crowds do come out and praise him. But he rides on a donkey, and even here has to face controversy: some of the Pharisees are unhappy and demand that Jesus control his disciples. He refuses, but still the point is clear: his welcome into Jerusalem is far from unanimous. The true king comes to claim his city, but does so in humility and weakness, showing his glory in a manner that leaves everyone free to choose how to respond.

John's understanding of Jesus' glory

In John's Gospel, Jesus' glory is seen primarily in his death on the cross. This is a clear manifestation of glorious weakness, and is a theme that runs right through the gospel. Jesus' glorious weakness is seen in the opening verses of the gospel, in the word made flesh, who leaves the eternal glory of heaven in order to dwell as a human being on earth (1:1-14). John's gospel is a witness to Jesus' glory, a glory he shows both in how he lives and also much more in how he dies.

Signs of God's glory

The first part of the Fourth Gospel (chapters 2-11) is sometimes described as 'the book of signs.' It contains seven 'signs' or miracles that demonstrate Jesus' glorious weakness. The fact that the signs are often misunderstood, or even pass unnoticed, can be taken as an indication that the glory shown is one of weakness, not of triumphalism. For example, the first sign, that of turning water into wine, is recognised by Jesus' disciples, but the majority of those present simply enjoy the results without thinking about the cause (2:11). Equally, the man by the pool is healed, but does not put his faith in Jesus (5:1-15). Thousands are fed from one boy's meal, but their response is not to glorify Jesus and worship him, but rather to attempt to make him king, arguably exactly what Jesus wishes to avoid, which is why he retreats up the mountain to be alone (6:1-15).

Undoubtedly there are clear signs of Jesus' divinity and glory: he heals with a word (4:43-54); walks on water (6:16-21); heals the man born blind, who does have faith in him (9:1-41); and raises Lazarus from the dead (11:38:43). Both the first sign of turning water into wine, and the seventh, of raising Lazarus, are linked to the glory of God (2:11; 11:40). Both are recognised by some, and rejected by others (the Pharisees' response to Lazarus' return to life is to plot to kill Jesus, 11:45-49). Jesus' glory is thus clearly displayed for those who have eyes to see, but where hearts are hardened, it is rejected. In this sense it is weak, as it is not coercive or forceful, but humble and open to rejection.

The glory of the Father and the Son

One of Jesus' primary concerns in John's Gospel is that of bringing glory to his Father. He says he does not want glory for himself, but rather for the one who sent him (8:50). Thus when he enters Jerusalem in triumph, he calls on his Father to glorify himself, and the Father responds, saying he will glorify his name (12:28). Even when more people follow Jesus, and grow in their relationship with him, this results in glory to the Father, not to Jesus (15:8).

Jesus understands the different ways in which glory is used: thus he castigates the unbelieving Jews for their concern with getting glory from each other, and their failure to seek God's glory (5:44). I would suggest these two understandings of glory are the 'triumphalist' and the 'weak' understandings I have been comparing in this chapter. The Jews are seeking glory in the triumphalist sense of personal acclaim and acknowledgement, getting a good reputation. Jesus rejects this, preferring to seek only the glorious weakness of his Father, which is why he does not accept glory from human beings, especially from those who don't have God's love in their hearts (5:41).

This contrast is mentioned another time in the Fourth Gospel. Jesus compares those who speak for their own gain and personal glory with those who choose to do the Father's will and seek his glory (7:18). This latter group will be self-effacing, and could appear weak. In the discussion from which this quote is taken, Jesus is accused of being a deceiver (7:12) and demon-possessed (7:20), showing how glorious weakness is easily misunderstood.

The concern for glory is in a sense mutual. When Jesus prays in the garden of Gethsemane, he prays that the Father will glorify the Son, so that the Son may bring glory to the Father (17:1). Although there is a mutual concern, it is also clear that the Father is the source of all glory, and that he has first given glory to the Son, which the Son then returns (17:4, 5, 10, 22, 24). This glory is the manifestation of God's character, the recognition of who he is, and so can still be understood as glorious weakness. The mutual interdependence of the Father and the Son is hinted at elsewhere in John's Gospel (e.g. 15:9-10); here it is understood using the idea of glory.

Isaiah's vision of Jesus' glory

Perhaps one of the harder texts to understand in John's Gospel in relation to glory is the claim in 12:41 that Isaiah saw Jesus' glory and spoke about him. But how did Isaiah see Jesus when he lived hundreds of years before him?

In the verse that comes before this statement, John has just quoted two areas of Isaiah's ministry, one about the servant being glorified and lifted in suffering (12:38; Isaiah 52:13-53:12) and the other a scene of glory in the temple (12:39-40; Isaiah 6:1-10). Early Christians linked Isaiah 6:1 with 52:13, because both texts use the phrase 'exalted and lifted up', and they also noted how 6:1 speaks of God, and so concluded that Jesus' lifting up by crucifixion was the point at which his identity as God was revealed. Those who did not believe were more concerned with human glory (i.e. triumphalist praise) and so failed to recognise the glorious weakness that the divine Jesus displayed. This is why their eyes are blinded, their hearts are hard and they fail to see clearly who Jesus is or what he has done for them.

The Son of God is lifted up in glorious weakness

As I said at the start of this section on John's Gospel, Jesus' death is understood as the primary display of his glory. Jesus' death is described as being 'lifted up', and compared with the incident in Numbers 21:4-9 where

Moses lifted up a bronze snake on a pole, a sign that all could see. All who turned to that lifted up snake and believed would be saved; in the same way, all who turn to the lifted up Jesus and believe will also be saved (3:14-15). Jesus is to be lifted up to draw all people to himself (12:32).

Death by crucifixion is a clear display of weakness, but also it is the means by which God displays his glory to the world. This is prefigured in Jesus' actions in washing his disciples' feet (13:1-17). When they gathered for the final meal together, none of them would take on the lowliest of tasks, that of washing one another's feet. It was a task no free man could be compelled to do for another, a job left to servants or slaves. Yet Jesus, entirely of his own free will, chooses to humble himself by stripping off his outer clothing and washing his disciples' feet. The conversation with Peter helps to clarify what is taking place: this is not simply a ritual of cleansing, but a challenge regarding participation and acceptance of what Jesus has done for us. Those who rely on their own efforts to clean themselves cannot benefit from this washing, and it must be accepted on Jesus' own terms, rather than on ones we dictate. This is a clear display within John's Gospel of the glorious weakness of the Son of God, who holds his status lightly: he is clear that he is the one in authority ('You call me "Teacher" and "Lord" and rightly so, for that is what I am,' 13:13) and yet also he is the one who is prepared to serve even the lowliest of people, even Judas, who was about to go out to betray him.

Jesus, glorious in weakness

Throughout this chapter I have tried to show how Jesus is not concerned with triumphalism, with developing a reputation or receiving praise from human beings. His only concern is doing his Father's will. His glory is seen in his humility, his weakness and humble service. He is building an alternative empire, challenging the religious and political hierarchies of his day, demonstrating that there is a different way to live, an alternative understanding of glory. His followers accepted this challenge to live out lives of glorious weakness. The Apostle Paul provides us with the clearest paradigm to follow, and so it is to his life we turn, looking first at Paul the Apostle of Glorious Weakness before expounding the theme of cruciform imitation of Christ.

Paul the Apostle of Glorious Weakness

So far our discussion of glorious weakness has been largely theoretical: we have seen glorious weakness as the controlling idea running through the Bible's account of God's dealing with his people; and we have looked at how Jesus perfectly displayed glorious weakness in his life and death. Now I'd like to move on from theological thought to decisive action. Richard Hays comments that one thing he has leant from the Radical Reformers is that 'theological thought can never be separated from its embodiment in concrete communities of worship and service.'[12] Christianity is not a theory to be contemplated, but a life to be lived. The apostle Paul learnt how to live a life of glorious weakness, and commends this life to all those who would follow after Christ. This life of weakness is one where personal goals and ambitions are surrendered, and concern for God's glory and the good of others becomes paramount. Christianity was therefore not something that could be practised in isolation, but something that must be lived out in community. Weakness was something Paul freely chose to display to others, in spite of the misinterpretation and suffering that resulted.

12   Hays, 'Embodying the Gospel in Community', quote from page 577.

In the first century Roman and Greek worlds – much as today – the idea of weakness was one that was greeted with contempt and intimidation, not with recognition or respect. People who showed any kind of weakness were looked down upon as failures, not worthy of any real attention. In this world that prioritised strength, Judaism had a different opinion. The Psalmist noted God's concern for the weak and the poor, as for example in Psalm 12:

> 'Help, LORD, for the godly are no more; the faithful have vanished from among men. Everyone lies to his neighbour; their flattering lips speak with deception. May the LORD cut off all flattering lips and every boastful tongue that says, "We will triumph with our tongues; we own our lips—who is our master?" "Because of the oppression of the weak and the groaning of the needy, I will now arise," says the LORD. "I will protect them from those who malign them." And the words of the LORD are flawless, like silver refined in a furnace of clay, purified seven times. O LORD, you will keep us safe and protect us from such people forever. The wicked freely strut about when what is vile is honoured among men.

What is interesting about this Psalm is the recognition that the order of the Graeco-Roman world, where might was right, is one that the Psalmist also sees around about him. But even though that is the reality he is confronted with, his theological foundations are strong enough that he realises this is not the true picture: those who are weak will ultimately be defended and protected by God, even if their present situation remained one of oppression and suffering.[13] A life of weaknesses is therefore the best choice; it is the only way God's glory can be made known to the world.

Paul worked with both parts of this framework: he understood and supported divine compassion for the poor, but also had to confront and challenge a triumphalist theology that saw glory as domination, and faith in Christ as a life of victory and superiority. This is especially notable in his correspondence with the church in Corinth. This was because of the characteristics of Corinth as a city. As Ben Witherington puts it:

> 'Corinth was a city where public boasting and self-promotion had become an art form. The Corinthian people lived within an honour-shame culture cultural orientation, where public recognition was often more important than facts and were the worst thing that could happen was for one's reputation to be publicly tarnished. In such a culture a person's sense of worth is based on recognition by others of one's accomplishments.'[14]

Corinth was a port city, rebuilt as a Roman colony on the orders of Julius Caesar in 44BC. It was full of up-and-coming people who had got rich quick and now wanted to stay rich and at the top of the social tree. Paul's normal mode of operation sat very uncomfortably

13 The theme of God's care for the weak reoccurs regularly in the Psalms. See for example Psalm 9:18; 14:6; 22:26; 113:7; 140:12. Some of the ideas for this section are based on Ehrensperger, *Paul and the dynamics of power: communication and interaction in the early Christ-movement*, chapter 6.

14 Witherington, *Conflict and Community*, page 8.

with such an elite. The basic problem came from the fact that Paul worked with his hands, supporting his work as a teacher and apostle of Christ by making tents. Well-to-do aristocratic Romans and Greeks often had a low opinion of those who practiced a trade. This meant many of Paul's problems in Corinth seem to have been caused by the wealthy and the social climbers among the Corinthians who were upset at him for not meeting their expectations for a great orator and teacher. Corinth was a city where an enterprising person could rise quickly in society through the accumulation and judicious use of newfound wealth. It seems that in Paul's time many in Corinth were suffering from a self-made-person-escapes-humble-origins syndrome: 'In a city where social climbing was a major preoccupation, Paul's deliberate stepping down in apparent status would have been seen by many as disturbing, disgusting, and even provocative.'[15]

In the face of a repeated emphasis on power, wealth and authority, Paul very deliberately emphasises weakness and suffering. This isn't a way of going behind the back of those addressed or making a hidden bid for power. Rather Paul sees this as the only way by which he can remind the Corinthians of the radical nature of life in Christ, and the freedom that it brings from all the trappings of power and authority that were in operation in first-century Corinth.

Paul does not set out a 'doctrine' of weakness, nor does he claim that weakness is an essential pre-requisite of faith in Christ. But he does not shy away from it, and he commends a life of weakness as one that powerfully and clearly embodies the gospel and so portrays the glory

15 Witherington, *Conflict and Community*, page 20.

of God to all who witness it. Paul's main discussion of weakness comes throughout his letters to the Corinthians and seems to be a response to criticisms from his opponents regarding his own weakness. David Alan Black identifies three sub-themes in Paul's understanding of weakness: anthropological; Christological; and ethical. We shall look at each in turn.[16]

The anthropological aspect of weakness

Black suggests that Paul's weakness motif is first of all *anthropological* because it presupposes that human beings are entirely dependent upon God and that human beings, created by God, are susceptible to the limitations of all creation. Human beings have limits, and it is proper that we recognise this reality. To an extent, human weakness is a sign of human participation in the old age, and so is associated with, if not strictly identified with 'flesh' and sinful tendencies. Paul describes the Roman Christians as 'weak in their flesh' or in their 'natural selves', having had a tendency to choose to sin before they came to Christ (Rom. 6:19).

Sadly this human weakness does not end when we come to faith in Christ. Paul knows, for example, that we are often weak and unclear as to what to pray for, or unable to pray effectively (Rom. 8:26). This is a reminder of human impotence and inability to do anything to please God, and makes it clear just how much we need God. But our inability means that times of prayer can become the

16 What follows is based on Black, *Paul, Apostle of Weakness*, pages 222-245.

very place in which the help and power of God are fully expressed.

Weakness in prayer is one place to experience God's glory, but for Paul, it was his illness that became the key place for experience of the power and grace of the Lord (2 Cor. 12:7-10). His illness keeps him from boasting in his revelations (12:7); enables him to experience the power of Christ (12:9); and teaches him the true purpose of hardships, persecutions and personal difficulties (12:10).

Paul understands that the weaknesses of humanity cannot be avoided in this present life, but they will all be eradicated in the kingdom. At the same time, weakness is also the platform from which the power of God is exhibited to the world, a point that is nowhere emphasised more clearly than in the cross of Christ.

> 'From a purely human perspective, the suffering and death of Christ appeared to be powerlessness and foolishness (1 Cor 1:25, 27); but God was at work in Christ's weakness, revealing in it the ultimate display of power by raising him from the dead (2 Cor 13:4).'[17]

The Christological aspect of weakness

Paul's understanding of weakness can be said to be Christological – indeed, Christ-centred – because he understands everything in terms of his relationship with Christ. As Paul sees it, although human beings are weak, in the very impotence and mortality of human beings there

17 Black, *Paul, Apostle of Weakness*, page 235.

is concealed the resurrection power of God, operative both in the life of the church (e.g. Acts 4:7, 33; 6:8) and in the life of every believer (e.g. Phil. 4:13; Col. 1:11). The most succinct statement of this is found in 2 Corinthians 12:9:

> But he said to me, "My grace is sufficient for you, for my power is made perfect in weakness." Therefore I will boast all the more gladly about my weaknesses, so that Christ's power may rest on me.

Black summarises the point clearly:

> 'Paul is well content with weaknesses, not because they are desirable in and of themselves, but because they are the vehicle through which the all-sufficient power of his Lord becomes prominent. *Human weakness paradoxically provides the best opportunity for divine power.* It is this principle that makes weakness more meaningful to Paul than to his opponents or even his converts. Whenever he feels himself to be weak – a fragile earthen vessel, persecuted, insulted, beset with afflictions of every kind – he feels Christ's strength. ... In itself, weakness indicates that Paul is still a part of the created order and that he awaits ultimate redemption; but when weakness becomes a means by which the Lord exercises his power, it shows that God's might has indeed manifested itself in the world through the death and resurrection of Christ, thereby overcoming the inability of the law and the flesh (Rom 5:6; 8:3).'[18]

Paul is clear that the Gospel is a message of foolishness, one of weakness and shame that ultimately leads to glory

18   Black, *Paul, Apostle of Weakness*, pages 237-238.

and triumph (1 Cor 1:18-25). Paul wants us all to recognise the weakness of Christ, who 'was crucified in weakness, but lives by the power of God.' (2 Cor. 13:4).

The ethical aspect of weakness

Paul firmly believes that the church should be a place of weakness. Twice he refers to the weak in the church who lack the full knowledge of faith, expressed in ascetic and legalistic behaviour (Rom. 14; 1 Cor. 8). Paul is sympathetic regarding their concerns, but is also clear that these people need to grow in maturity; yet they are welcome in the Christian community, and must not be condemned but encouraged. This aspect of Paul's teaching grows out of his teaching about the reciprocal, mutually edifying love that should exist between believers. Christians are members together of the body of Christ, and as brothers and sisters they are to live together in a spirit of mutual dependence and unity, serving each other in love (Gal. 5:13) and in oneness of soul and purpose (Phil 2:1-2).

Paul does not teach against Christian liberty, but rather argues that the Christian must exercise his liberty before God on the basis of whatever is good for the whole community, and not just himself. This is also clear in the teaching on the use of spiritual gifts: thus 1 Corinthians 13 is placed between chapters 12 and 14 to make it clear that a spiritual gift in and of itself has no value, since the essential question is whether or not the gift edifies the church as it is exercised in love. Those who have the more conspicuous gifts have a correspondingly greater duty to foster unity within the church.

Paul's weakness in 2 Corinthians

I will develop these themes further in the next section, which builds on these ideas to develop an understanding of 'cruciform imitation', copying Christ's willingness to be crucified. For the moment I will return to 2 Corinthians to examine further Paul's understanding of weakness. I will look at two sections, 4:1-12 and 11:16-12:10, as Paul spells out what it means to live a gloriously weak life.

2 Corinthians 4

The writer Bill Lyon suggests an interesting philosophy on life. He says, 'If at first you don't succeed, find out if the loser gets anything.' Obviously he meant it as a joke, but the thing Christians know is that actually the loser does get something. This is the point that Paul wants us to understand: that it is the weak, the failures, that God uses to display his glory to the world.

When we talk about weakness, the gospel of fragility and vulnerability, there are two equal but opposite dangers. The first is that we can stray into masochism and the second is to deny all weakness. The first view says if it doesn't hurt, then its not of God. And that's not true. It is true that discipleship is costly. As Jesus himself said, if anyone would follow after me, he must take up his cross, which means, if I want to follow Jesus, I must die to myself and my own ambitions. But I don't need to be a masochist. I don't need to beat myself up with my weaknesses. But equally, I shouldn't ignore my weaknesses and claim that I don't have any, that faith in Christ has solved all my problems. Some of us tend to be overly hard on ourselves. Others tend to be overly kind. We need to listen and learn from Paul what it means to recognise that none of us is perfect, and learn how to live with this reality.

We're looking at 2 Corinthians 4 to see what we can learn about glorious weakness. At the close of chapter 3, Paul has been talking about how those who have faith in Christ are being transformed more and more into the likeness of Christ, and so he writes that 'the Lord, who is the Spirit, transforms us into his likeness in an ever greater degree of glory' (3:18). And its because of this, because we are being transformed into his glory that we are not discouraged, and we accept the work that God has given us to do.

And the attitude that we take when we follow God and do as he asks is really important. This is the attitude that Paul sets out in 4:2: 'Rather, we have renounced secret and shameful ways; we do not use deception, nor do we distort the word of God. On the contrary, by setting forth the truth plainly we commend ourselves to every man's conscience in the sight of God.'

What does he mean? Putting aside all secret and shameful deeds means not hiding anything away, but living a completely open life, a transparent life. It's very easy to put on a public face, to pretend everything is okay, when in fact its not. Adrian Plass tells a story about people coming to church every week, each holding a bag which they claim is full of faith, and presenting shiny, happy faces as they talk with each other and pretend everything is ok. But one week, when they have to actually open the bags of faith, they find they're all empty, and the shiny, happy faces are simply masks they put on to act out the 'successful Christian', when in reality they're hurt and broken inside.

Now of course, we have to be appropriate in our relationships, and find the right time to admit weakness and failure. But also we have to admit that we are weak and we do fail. What Paul is telling us to do in this verse is to be honest about everything that goes on in our lives, but to disown the rubbish, not to try and hide it. If you keep sweeping things under the carpet, sooner or later you'll have a real mess to deal with. A life of glorious weakness is not a morbid life, consumed by gloom or failure. But neither is it a deluded life, refusing to recognise the existence of any problems.

Paul knows what grace means: that even though he's failed, God still loves him and cares for him. And that means his failures don't really matter. Most of us, I think, find failure really hard to deal with, and so would rather pretend it didn't happen. I learnt this about myself when I was doing my minibus driving tests. The fact that it is 'tests' and not 'test' makes the point. It took me three attempts to pass, because in the first two each time I did one silly thing. The first time, I got too close to a cyclist, who swerved when he saw me, and so that was a dangerous fault and I failed. The second time I can't even remember what I did. I think it was that my road position was a bit dodgy once, and so I slowed traffic coming the opposite way. But that meant I failed twice, which I still don't really like admitting. But I think its good for me to do so. I think we have to admit our weaknesses, the things we do wrong, the things we're scared of and so on. That's what makes us recognisably human. And most of all, its our human weaknesses that God can really use. That is the point Paul is making in 2 Corinthians 4.

In 4:2 he tells us to live in the light of truth: to admit when we're wrong and to live in the light. And he warns us why it won't be easy. In verse four, Paul tells us how the god of this age has blinded the eyes of those who don't believe. I don't think he's talking about the devil (why would Paul say the devil was a god?). More likely he's talking about anything that the rightful place of God. Every generation and every place has its own idols. For many people in the city where I live, Liverpool, its probably football. There are loads of other things that we make gods in our lives – success, money, power, relationships, sex, a good job, holidays, kids doing well at school or work and so on. Paul tells us that whatever it is, what we need is for the light of God to break in; for blind eyes to be opened and for each of us to be able to see the light of the Good News of the Glory of Christ. God is the one who can bring light into our dark situations, and help us to truly see.

And when the light shines on us, what we truly see is what Paul says in verses seven to twelve:

> 'But we have this treasure in jars of clay to show that this all-surpassing power is from God and not from us. We are hard pressed on every side, but not crushed; perplexed, but not in despair; persecuted, but not abandoned; struck down, but not destroyed. We always carry around in our body the death of Jesus, so that the life of Jesus may also be revealed in our body. For we who are alive are

always being given over to death for Jesus' sake, so
that his life may be revealed in our mortal body.
So then, death is at work in us, but life is at work
in you.'

The reference to 'jars of clay' means the disposable plates
of the day. Clay was a cheap material that you made the
most basic, simple things out of. Nothing special, nothing
important. Like disposable plates or cheap plastic cups.
Something that does a functional job and that's about it.
Apparently the Corinthians specialised in making a really
really thin kind of clay – so thin that you could put a lamp
inside the clay pot, and the light would shine through it,
and so you could use it to find your way around at night.
Its possible that Paul is referring to this, but he may simply
have ordinary clay pots in mind.

At any rate, his point is a very blunt assessment about
humanity – we're just common clay pots. Nothing
particularly special. Remember my earlier point about
us deceiving ourselves. Elsewhere Paul tells us to look at
ourselves with sober judgement, to assess realistically who
we are and what God is calling us to do: not being too
harsh, and equally not being too soft. When we get this
realistic assessment of ourselves right, then we also realise
that we have a treasure of unrivalled value – the most
valuable treasure we could possibly own – the supreme
power of God that is at work within us.

Its a bit like he's saying, each of us here is a common
clay pot, cracked and so a bit useless. But it's because its
cracked that the light of the good news of the glory of
Christ can shine through each of us. When we put on the
'I'm perfect' mask, we block up all the cracks, and so we

hide all the light. Its only when we admit weakness and failure that the light of Jesus shines through the cracks.

And that is exactly the point Paul is making in 4:10-12. This is the heart of Paul's understanding of Christian faith and life. We all carry about the death of Jesus in the body so that the life of Jesus may also be revealed.

Sounds great, but what does it mean? Well, when Paul says 'we all carry about the death of Jesus in our mortal bodies,' I think he's picking up on an image he uses in 1 Corinthians 12, that the church is the body of Christ. So what he means is that the church, to function properly as the church, must be irrevocably marked by the death of Jesus. Unless we die with Christ, we cannot truly live. That's why he says in verse 11, 'throughout our lives we are always in danger of death for Jesus' sake, in order that his life may also be seen in our bodies.' In our Christian lives we must be marked as much by Jesus' death as by his life. But what does that mean?

Well, put simply, what it means is that we need to recognise that we're not very good at running our own lives. That because we're so far short of perfect, what we really need to do is let ourselves, our desires to be in control, to do things our way die. Let all of that die, and so make space for the light of Jesus to shine in and through our lives. As Jesus said, if anyone would follow after me, he must take up his cross – which means, must choose to die. And that is what we should do. Paul is clear that when we die to ourselves, when we admit completely our weakness and failure, then and only then can God really work powerfully in and through us. This is a point that he makes very clearly later on in the letter, when he becomes a lot more personal in his discussion.

2 Corinthians 11:16-12:10

The second part of 2 Corinthians I'm going to focus on specifically is the section where Paul responds to the accusation that he's not up to much as an apostle. The situation appears to be something like this: after Paul left Corinth, various people turned up and started ministering amongst the new Christians there. Part of their work was no doubt positive, but they over emphasised visions and personal experience of God, putting too much stress on charismatic worship. They also appear to have been very self-confident, and proud of who they were. Paul responds to all of this, first by defending his own ministry, what he had done, and second by comparing himself with these other teachers, whom he calls 'false apostles.' I'm going to pick up his argument part way through in 11:16, and work through it in short sections. As in the earlier section, Paul again argues that glorious weakness is the only way to live a godly life.

11:16-21 He begins by telling the Corinthian Christians that he's going to boast like other fools to show how foolish those who are calling him foolish are, i.e. he'll play the fools at their own game to show what a foolish game it is, and what fools they are to play it. So for the sake of his argument, Paul casts himself not as an apostle any longer, but as a fool, so he boasts just as these others are boasting.

Glorious Weakness

He then mocks the Corinthians – they are so intelligent, they can happily cope with such foolishness, although they themselves have been the fools to allow themselves to be exploited by the newcomers, who appear to be exerting complete control over the Corinthians. Paul's irony continues – he was too weak to be so exploitative – but now he will play them at their own game.

11:22 These men, like Paul, are clearly Jews of impeccable pedigree. The first three comparisons:

Hebrews are they?   *So am I, says Paul.*

Israelites are they?   *So am I, says Paul.*

Abraham's seed are they?   *So am I, says Paul.*

11:23   But the fourth comparison:

Ministers of Christ are they?   I am better!

And how Paul is better is striking: he has faced worse and suffered more than they.

11:24-29 Paul has suffered at the hands of all kinds of people; Jews and Romans, stoning, shipwrecks and so on. Even his constant travels mean he is always in danger, as roads were rarely safe places to be – there were the risks both from robbers and also from flooded or swollen rivers. He also faced opposition from both Jews and Gentiles, wherever he found himself. Paul's determination not to be a burden to the churches means he has had to work especially hard – his trade was repairing tents, and he had to do this around his work as a preacher and teacher.

But Paul's biggest pressure come from his concern for the churches he was responsible for.

Paul is clear that he enjoyed his ministry, and was grateful to God for the converts he saw, but that does not deny the pressure he faced. Paul pastorally identifies himself with those he cared for, and so suffered as they experienced pressure and failure.

11:30-33 These are the only things that Paul will boast in: the suffering and pressure he has experienced as a result of his calling to be the Apostle to the Gentiles. Paul knows, as a Christian and a Hebrew, that he is being truthful before God – and that his honesty is a challenge to those he is now opposing. Paul closes with an example of the pressure he faced and the weakness of his ministry – soon after his conversion, he had to flee Damascus, and the only way he managed to do it was by being lowered down the wall in a bucket, hardly the mark of a triumphant leader!

This is Paul's list of achievements: the number of times he has been beaten, stoned, shipwrecked, mugged, hungry, thirsty, cold, stressed and troubled by other people. Have you ever heard anyone else talk in this way? There is a certain machismo that boasts in endurance, (number of miles run/weights lifted/hours worked etc.) but Paul's experience is both qualitatively and quantitively different from our daily experience. When we talk about what we have achieved in church, or how successful we are at ministry, it is always about good things. This is natural, and Christianity in no way condones or promotes a masochistic view of life. But that doesn't mean we should ignore the challenge of Paul's experience and his dedication to Jesus regardless of personal cost.

In a sense, Paul's ministry is successful precisely because of the amount of anguish and pain that he experienced. He cares deeply for those in his charge – and so suffers for them; he cares deeply for those who never accept Jesus, and so is prepared to endure much that they might have a chance to hear. Successful ministry is never going to be easy: we must be prepared for the cost. As Luther is reputed to have said, 'If Christ wore a crown of thorns, why do his followers expect to wear a crown of roses?'

12:1-6 And this is exactly the point that Paul carries on developing: he's not yet done boasting. First of all he makes it clear that as well as having as good a lineage as those he's challenging, he's also had as good, if not better, set of charismatic experiences. Paul narrates the ascent of 'a man in Christ' to the 'third heaven'. Since this vision is one that could be told to no one, it must be Paul's own experience – he is ironically distancing himself from this experience of 'power' because it is irrelevant. Although Paul could boast about that, where he would not be called a fool, he chooses to return back to the foolish boasting regarding his weakness, since such personal experiences are irrelevant for his ministry. This is a really interesting point – it is not the mountain-top experiences of God that makes a successful Christian, but the mess of daily life, of proclaiming the good news of Jesus Christ in the midst of personal weakness and failure that is the source of our real strength and power.

12:7-10 In order to prevent over-exaltation, Paul is given this 'thorn', which torments him. The 'thorn' could be relational (the growing opposition to his ministry) or it could be physical (the popular suggestion is short-sightedness or blindness, based on Paul's comment to the Galatians that they would have gladly torn out their eyes for him). I think the Holy Spirit has made sure we don't know exactly what it was, so this passage can speak all the more powerfully to each one of us. Whatever the thorn was, Paul asked for it to be removed – 'three times' may be symbolic of repeated prayer. So Paul kept asking God for a solution, and eventually he received his answer from God – perhaps both personally and also by reflecting further on Jesus' life and ministry. And the answer was this: Christ's death and life are reproduced in the lives of his people. God's power that is made perfect through Christ's weakness in death by crucifixion is then shown to the world in the crucifixion of Paul's inflated pride through this 'thorn'. All of us – whatever power we have: intelligence, wealth, influence, or position – sooner or later become powerless and vulnerable. When such people in their powerlessness (whether bodily, relational, financial or structural) call out to the Lord, the grace of Christ is shown and the power of Christ rests on them.

Because of this, Paul will therefore boast all the more of his weaknesses, and indeed even take pleasure in them, because it is through them, and not through his vision that took him to the third heaven, that he experiences the true power of Christ. Christ's sufferings are replicated and extended in the sufferings of his Apostle as he bids humanity to be reconciled with God – and this is the source of Paul's pleasure and purpose in life.

Paul, gloriously weak

Paul knows when he is weak, then he is strong. Weakness creates the human context of helplessness and utter vulnerability in which Paul pleads with the risen powerful Lord, who was himself once weak, sin-laden and poor, but now is strong in resurrection power, and gives power and grace to all those who call out to him. That's the point that Paul would have us remember: it's only when you can't do it, and you know you can't do it, that you know Jesus can, and does, do it. Paul modelled his own life, and wants all Christians to model their lives, on the life of Jesus. We have seen in the previous chapter how Jesus lived a life of glorious weakness, and we have seen in this chapter how Paul lived as an apostle of weakness. We turn in our next chapter to the topic of cruciform imitation, of living a life of glorious weakness patterned after Jesus' life, which was focussed entirely on his death on the cross.

Cruciform Imitation

So far I have traced the theme of glorious weakness through the story of the Bible, and have looked in some detail at Jesus and Paul, noting how their lives were characterised by glorious weakness. This has given us a lot to copy as we try to live gloriously weak lives. We're going to look now in some more detail at Paul's instructions regarding 'cruciform imitation,' how we can copy the life of Jesus that is indelibly marked by his cross. I've already suggested that Jesus' death on the cross is the ultimate display of glorious weakness, and so throughout this chapter I will simply assume that a pattern of cruciform imitation is one of glorious weakness.

A number of times throughout his letters, Paul explicitly instructs his audience to imitate his Christian life, whilst at other times the instruction is only implicit in what he says. In particular Paul encourages his audience to imitate him as he imitates Christ. As well as this he also recommends other models of Christian conduct, such as Timothy. Paul uses himself as an example of Christian conduct right through his first letter to the Corinthians, and we will follow the usage there in order to outline some of the main elements of his understanding of imitation.

Paul's Personal Example in 1 Corinthians

Paul held the church in Corinth in a great deal of affection, even though they caused him quite a few problems. He wrote a number of long letters to them, of which only two survive in the New Testament today. As we noted in the previous chapter, Corinth was a young, up-and-coming city, in which the pushy and the arrogant could make quick money. It was a city where rhetoric and public speaking skills were prized, and where people aligned themselves with, and imitated, the latest 'big name' teachers. It was also a city known for sexual immorality, especially through temple prostitutes associated with the cult of Aphrodite. There were thus many bad examples for the Corinthian Christians to copy, and so Paul sets out Christian alternatives to encourage them to stay on the straight and narrow. In particular he recommends his own conduct to them as a model to follow.

'Therefore I urge you to imitate me' (1 Corinthians 4:16)

Paul's use of himself as an example is seen his direct command in 4:16. The immediate context of this statement is Paul's observation that although the Corinthian Christians may have ten thousand guardians in Christ he, Paul, is their father in the faith (4:15). A father was the undisputed head of his household in both first-century Roman and Jewish society, and as such would command obedience from those within their family. So when Paul urges imitation of his pattern of Christian living, he is speaking from a position of loving authority. That is to say, he is speaking with the expectation of a father that his spiritual children will obey him, but also with an attitude of deep concern for the Corinthian Christians, as any loving father would have towards his children.

Paul has just set out the challenges and hardships he considers a normal part of an apostolic ministry (4:9-13). Apostles are public figures of shame, like condemned men who form the final figures in a parade into a Roman circus. They are foolish, weak, dishonoured, hungry, thirsty, badly clothed, ill treated and homeless. To a status conscious society like Corinth, Paul is effectively saying that being a leading follower of Christ meant you became the worst of the worst, a figure of shame and contempt. And yet he makes it clear to them that they should not be ashamed of what it means to be an apostle; on the contrary, it comes as a warning to his dear children about the reality of the Christian life, that it is not a life of self-exaltation or self-glorification, but rather one of humility, of emptying oneself in the service of others. And that is why Paul wants the Corinthian Christians to imitate him, so that their lives can also become Christ-like. As Michael Jensen puts it, what Paul is saying in 4:16 is that 'to imitate him is to imitate one who regards himself as lowly, even nothing; but to imitate one who is committed in love for the good of the other.'[19]

19   Jensen, 'Imitating Paul, imitating Christ', page 23.

Should I claim my rights?

One complex area that Paul spends quite a lot of 1 Corinthians discussing is the issue of whether Christians should use all of their rights, or whether they should renounce them for the sake of the Gospel. His fundamental argument is that Christians should renounce their rights, just as Christ renounced his. Paul presents himself as an example of this, an example he wants the Corinthian Christians to imitate.

In chapter six, Paul has been discussing the issue of lawsuits. He suggests that in order to present a good Christian witness it is better to suffer a legal injustice rather than take a fellow believer to court (6:1-8). He is referring primarily to property disputes and similar civil court cases rather than a serious criminal matter such as murder or rape. In Roman courts of the day, it was allowed (even expected) that those involved in the case could use their political, financial and social interests to influence the course of such trials. So Paul is saying that Christians should not exercise their rights to defend their own interests at the expense of others.

He introduces the concept of renunciation of rights as he makes it clear that those who live primarily for their own benefits, in whatever way that might be, have no chance of entering the kingdom of God (6:9-10). The Corinthians well know that 'that is what some of you were. But you were washed, you were sanctified, you were justified in the name of the Lord Jesus and by the Spirit of our God' (6:11).

Having made their new status as forgiven people clear, Paul then sets out to explain how this should lead to voluntary self-renunciation. Their Christian freedom is to be used primarily for the good of others. So in 6:12, he presents himself as an example of what it means to be a washed, sanctified, justified believer, who practises, 'self-limitation of freedom, self-disciple and a new-found ability to shun sinful behaviour,'[20] in this particular case, sexual immorality (6:13-20).

The point is developed in Paul's discussion of food sacrificed to idols and of his own ministry (chapters eight and nine, respectively). He warns that the exercise of Christian freedom must not become a stumbling block for the weak (8:9), before presenting himself as an example of one who has rights and chooses not to use them. Brian Dodd suggests what Paul is saying is this:

> 'Consider these two contradictory facts in my life: I am both self-sufficient and an apostle who has the right to support. You know that I am an apostle because I have seen the Lord and I am the founder of your church. You know apostles have the right to support for several reasons. This is the practice of the other apostles, notably the brothers of the Lord and Cephas [9.1-5]. You count Barnabas and me among them [9.6]. Soldiers, farmers, and shepherds have such a right to gain support [9.7]. The scriptures grant us this right [9.8-10]. It is well established that we have a right to support [9.11-12a]. And now this is the example we have set for you: *We have not made use of our own right!* [9.12b]. Let me add that the temple servants have a right to

20 Dodd, *Paul's paradigmatic 'I'*, page 87.

support from their work [9.13], and that the Lord himself has commanded that the churches support missionaries [9.14]. We have the strongest possible case for receiving material support from you, *but I have not laid claim to this right!* [9.15-18] For the sake of the gospel I give up my rights on behalf of any who may be 'weak' [9.16-22]. I exhort you to exercise this same self-control for the sake of the weak and for the sake of the gospel [9.23-27].'[21]

Paul makes the same point again in 10:23-33, leading to the same conclusion, that the Corinthian Christians should follow his example as he follows the example of Christ. This idea of the Corinthians Christians imitating Paul who himself imitates Christ is one that reoccurs at a number of points throughout his letters. The chain of imitation is an important part of Paul's understanding of discipleship. Paul presents himself as both parts of the paradigm: he is both imitator and imitated, and his ideal model is one where others do the same, always referring back ultimately to Christ. And when Paul imitates Christ he especially means following a 'cruciform pattern' which primarily seeks the good of others, not of self.[22]

It must be noted that although Paul does press for community solidarity, he does not equate that with complete uniformity of ethical understanding. Paul nowhere seeks to educate the consciences of the weak as to the mistaken nature of their position. Thus although he does clearly argue that idols have no status, and therefore to offer food to them is meaningless (1 Corinthians 8:4-

---

21 Dodd, *Paul's paradigmatic 'I'*, pages 101-102. His italics.
22 Jensen, 'Imitating Paul, imitating Christ', page 23.

6), this is addressed to the strong, telling them something that they are already aware of. The imperative is to seek the good of others, not to force others to become like oneself.

Thus Paul uses his own example to demonstrate how, although he is free in Christ and this means he holds to a number of ethical standards, such as the meaninglessness of food offered to idols, he will happily renounce such rights if that renunciation will benefit a fellow Christian. The primary concern is that all are enabled, insofar as it is possible, to follow after the pattern of Christ. As David Horrell notes, the unity of the community and solidarity for each other 'is to be sustained through fostering the kind of other-regard which allows such differences of conviction and practise to remain, though this other-regard requires that the practice of the strong be compromised insofar as it endangers the weak.'[23]

The image of the Body

The idea of renunciation of one's personal rights for the good of all lies behind the famous image of the church as the Body of Christ. This was a common image in Paul's day. It was used to express the idea that individuals were part of a larger social whole; to depict an ideal and balanced form of social organisation, and even to legitimate the social status quo and the position of the ruling elite, as in the classic tale recounted in Livy (*History* 2.32). Sent to quell dissension against the ruling classes among the Roman plebs, Menenius Agrippa compares the lower classes to the limbs of the body who might, like the plebs, object to

23   Horrell, *Solidarity and difference*, page 182.

labouring to provide nourishment for the apparently idle belly (the ruling classes). Yet the result would be sickness and death for the whole body, since the stomach provides, as well as receives, nourishment![24]

Paul was almost certainly aware of such understandings and use of the image of the body, and challenges them directly. As he sees it, the image of the body is not hierarchical. Rather, the differences between different body parts are mutually beneficial. He resorts to comedy to make his point: the idea of the whole body being simply a giant squashy eyeball, or a huge wax-filled ear is farcical (12:15).[25] Just as the individual parts of the body work together for the good of all, so Paul expects the Corinthian Christians to copy his example and work together for the good of all, not for their own personal benefit. In particular those who are strong should make sacrifices for their weaker Christian siblings. This is true Christian weakness in action, whether the strong become weak for the sake of the weak, and so the body of Christ remains united and displays the glory of God for all to see.

Not always a binding model

Although Paul does repeatedly recommend himself as a model of Christian conduct, he is aware that there are some aspects of his life that are particular to his own calling, and so cannot be imposed *carte blanche* on the

24 Horrel., *Solidarity and difference*, page 123.
25 Note the discussion in Jensen, 'Imitating Paul, imitating Christ', page 24. The comedy that Paul intends here becomes particularly clear when one discusses this passage with children.

entire Corinthian church. His discussion on marriage makes this point clear. Although he does personally wish everyone were single, and so able to devote full attention to service of the gospel, he recognises that each person has his or her own gift from God and must accept that and stay in the state they are in if at all possible, although even then he is prepared for an individual's circumstances to change if that becomes necessary (7:7-9).

Paul's example to the Corinthian Christians

We have seen a number of elements of Paul's strategy of imitation from 1 Corinthians. First the chain of imitation: Paul encourages his audience to imitate him as he in turn imitates Christ. Second this Christ-like pattern of imitation has a cruciform shape: it involves surrender of rights and a strong concern for the protection and care of those who are weak. Finally we note that Paul does not expect every detail of his life to be copied slavishly, but rather each must discern for themselves what it means to imitate Christ.

Imitate me as I imitate Christ

As David Horrell notes, in Paul's letters,

> 'The explicit calls to imitation of Christ, few as they are, are only the tip of a much larger iceberg. Indeed, the appeal to conform to the pattern of Christ's story of humiliation for the sake of others through to vindication is often conveyed indirectly, through the example of Paul, who considers his

own life and practice to mirror this christological paradigm.'[26]

Paul regularly encourages others to imitate him as he imitates Christ. His audience cannot imitate Christ directly, since they have never had a personal encounter with him. Indeed Paul himself has only had faith-filled encounters with the risen Jesus, but still has much greater personal knowledge of Christ that those he is addressing.[27] Paul's missionary strategy was always to win converts in areas where people had no knowledge of Christ. But how were they to learn how to live as Christians if they did not have any prior knowledge of who Jesus was and how he lived?

In such circumstances it appears that 'Paul's method of shaping a community was to gather converts around himself and by his own behaviour to demonstrate what he taught. In doing this, he followed a widely practiced method of his day particularly by moral philosophers.'[28] This is a strategy that could equally be employed by the church today. Paul tells his converts: imitate me as I imitate Christ; this is how to learn about how to live a Christian life.

The fruits of this method can be seen in particular in the Thessalonian letters. Paul begins his first letter to them by commending them for becoming 'imitators of us and of the Lord' (1:6). As Michael Jensen puts it, 'in imitating

26 Horrell, *Solidarity and difference*, page 241.
27 It is quite possible that Paul had opportunity to observe Jesus, when still the devout Pharisee Saul of Tarsus. See Wenham, *Paul: Follower or Founder?.*
28 See Dodd, *Paul's paradigmatic 'I'* page 214.

Paul and his friends, the Thessalonians were able to discern the pattern of life that was Christ's and so to effectively imitate Christ *via* this apostolic mediation.'[29] Notice that this pattern emerges in the context of suffering, both of the Thessalonian Christians (1 Thess. 1:6), and of Paul (1 Thess. 2:2; Acts 17:5-6), reinforcing my suggestion that imitating Paul as he imitates Christ means following a cruciform pattern.

Paul's practise of providing a model for imitation is referred to at a number of other points in the Thessalonian letters. In 1 Thess. 4:10-12 he encourages them to love their Christian siblings, before suggesting they 'make it your ambition to lead a quiet life, to mind your own business and to work with your hands, just as we told you, so that your daily life may win the respect of outsiders and so that you will not be dependent on anybody' (4:11-12). Imitation of Christ is thus practised in part for an evangelistic purpose, to present Christ to those who do not yet know him.

The second purpose mentioned in these verses is to remove the possibility of unhealthy dependence or becoming a burden. This is also something Paul makes two other references to having modelled before the Thessalonian believers (1 Thess. 2:1-12; 2 Thess. 3:6-13). Paul thus continually reminds those he is addressing of their need to put into practise what they saw him do.

29 Jensen, 'Imitating Paul, imitating Christ', page 25.

Imitation of Christ should have a cruciform pattern

In Colossians 3:13, Paul urges his audience to 'forgive as the Lord forgave you.' The Lord's forgiveness of the Colossians only came about as a result of Jesus' death and resurrection, and so Paul's point is that Christ's actions in bearing their sins, which led to their being forgiven, should be imitated by the Colossians and so they also should choose to forgive. As Jensen puts it,

> 'The event which is constitutive of the church's life is also to be the model of the church's mutual relationships. There is then, a christological vision at the heart of Paul's call to imitate Christ; which explains how it is indeed possible to imitate a model who is also held to be unique.'[30]

The cruciform pattern of Christ in Philippians

This cruciform pattern of imitation is perhaps seen most clearly in the argument of Philippians 2 and 3. Before he introduces his Christological hymn, Paul tells his audience that 'your attitude should be the same as that of Christ Jesus' (Philippians 2:5). Thus as the Philippian Christians celebrate the story of Jesus' voluntary descent to death and then ascent into glory, they are to conform their own character and practice to the example set for them in Christ, and 'thus cultivate the virtues embodied

---

30   Jensen, 'Imitating Paul, imitating Christ', page 22.

in him – humility, other-regard, confidence and joy in suffering and so on.'[31]

Paul puts himself forward as providing an example of how this imitation is to take place. We can thus see in Philippians 2 and 3 the twin elements of imitation having a cruciform pattern and imitation of Paul as he imitates Christ. It must be noted that only the first part of the christological hymn presents a pattern for imitation. Whilst it is technically true that since we are 'in Christ' we receive the benefits of his exaltation and glorification, this is not something we in any way seek to imitate or emulate.

Park has identified five elements of Christ's submission in 2:6-8, which he argues are also present in Paul's personal example in 3:4-11, and in so far as they can be discerned, in the examples of Timothy (2:19-24) and Epaphroditus (2:25-30). These five are forsaking rights; slavery/ servanthood and obedience; humility; humiliation and suffering; and volition.[32] I take these to be the five components of a gloriously weak life.

2:6-11 begins with Christ forsaking his rights. He is described as having equality with God, but he did not consider that to be something to be taken advantage of. Although he has certain rights, he decides not to use them. Thus equality with God does not become an occasion for self-advantage or self-promotion, but rather for self-

31 Horrell, *Solidarity and difference*, page 214.
32 What follows is based on Park, *Submission within the Godhead and the Church in the Epistle to the Philippians*, pages 120-123.

abnegation.[33] Christ who is in 'very nature' God chooses to take the 'very nature' of a slave, the one without any advantages, rights or privileges.

Second, the purpose of a slave is primarily to obey and to serve others. Christ's service is offered to all, and his obedience is complete, not conditional upon anything. He does not cease to obey when things become difficult, inconvenient or unjust. He chooses to obey in the face of suffering and humiliation, serving others with no thought of self.

Third, Christ's humility is seen in his decision to empty himself, to move from the position of highest privilege (equality with God), to the lowest possible, that of a slave, one completely stripped of all rights and privileges, at the beck and call of his master, one who is little more than a piece of property. This humility is underscored by the decision to obey even to death.

Fourth, the fact that Christ is obedient not simply to death, but even to death on a cross, signifies extreme humiliation and suffering. Crucifixion was an especially cruel form of punishment, forbidden to be used against Roman citizens. It could be prolonged for days, linked with other forms of torture, notably flogging, and entailed public humiliation and exposure, as those condemned were nailed naked to a cross, subject to the public ridicule and scorn of all as they slowly suffocated to death. Christ voluntarily choose to undergo this extreme humiliation and suffering.

33 Park, *Submission within the Godhead and the Church in the Epistle to the Philippians*, page 120.

This is the fifth point, that Christ's submission was voluntary. Free from any coercion or obligation, it was entirely self-willed. This must be understood in the context of Christ's equality with God. He voluntarily lays aside those rights, freely chooses the form of a servant and is obedient, even to the extreme of death by crucifixion.

Paul's imitation of Christ's cruciform pattern

These five elements of submission are also found in Paul's description of his own conduct, presented as an example for the Philippians to emulate. I would add that whilst all five elements are present, there is a marked difference between Jesus' submission and that practised by human beings. The distinctions will be noted throughout the discussion that follows.[34]

First we note that just as Christ forsakes the rights, status and privileges of being equal with God, so too Paul lays down his own rights, status and privileges (Phil. 3:4-9). Of course, Paul's privileges are entirely human, and so incomparable with those of Christ. But Paul is, nevertheless, a man of impeccable Jewish pedigree. The point of the comparison is that both Paul and Christ have voluntarily forsaken rights, status and privileges that they could have chosen to use for their own personal advantage.

Paul's lack of concern for his own advantage is seen elsewhere in Philippians. A prisoner, subject to jealous rivalry from other believers, and even facing the possibility

---

34 What follows is based on Park, *Submission within the Godhead and the Church in the Epistle to the Philippians*, pages 124-127.

of death, Paul shifts away from focusing on his own predicament and centres his attention of the possibility of glorifying Christ in these circumstances (1:20). His concern for others over his own benefit is also seen in 1:22-26, where Paul makes it clear that his personal desire to die and be with Christ is of lesser importance than the benefit of the Philippians. Furthermore, he is prepared to not only devote his life to them, but even to be poured out as a sacrifice together with them (2:17-18).

Second, Paul introduces himself to the Philippians as the slave of Christ (1:1), one whose purpose is to serve not his own will, but that of Christ. The same point is implicit in the discussion in 3:7-11, where Paul spells out in more detail his total dedication to obey the call God has placed on his life. Park also suggests that Paul's renunciation of the privileges of his heritage (a Hebrew of the tribe of Benjamin, a zealous Pharisee etc) is a further indication of Paul's obedience to God's standards as opposed to his own or any other human standard.[35]

This renunciation of privilege indicates Paul's humility before God and humans. Whilst he could have claimed the benefits of his status, Paul voluntary strips himself of all these in recognition that any human accomplishment before God is simply rubbish (3:7-8). There is a qualitative difference between the humility displayed by Christ and that shown by Paul. Christ's humility is voluntary, but unnecessary in light of his equality with God. By contrast, for human beings, humility is always both the indispensable and the entirely appropriate attitude one should adopt

---

35 Park, *Submission within the Godhead and the Church in the Epistle to the Philippians*, page 127.

before God. Although humility is a necessary prerequisite for human beings to enter into right relationship with God, nevertheless it is an attitude that must be chosen voluntarily. An element of selflessness must be taken up freely; one Paul does through his obedience and adoption of the role of slave before God (1:1).

Fourth, Paul also undergoes humiliation and suffering. Indeed, Paul believes that salvation leads not only to the blessings of grace (2:1-2) but also to participation in humiliation and suffering, which he regards not as disadvantages, but as privileges of faith in Christ (1:29). His understanding that humiliation and suffering are privileges is seen in his embracing of his imprisonment (1:12-14) and of the injury inflicted on him by fellow believers taking advantage of his situation (1:15-18). He is even willing to surrender his own life both for the sake of the Philippian Christians (1:22-26; 2:17) and for Christ (1:19-22).

Finally, as with Christ, there is no evidence that Paul's submission was a result of oppression or coercion. Rather, Paul willingly forsakes his rights, privileges and status (3:4-8); he willingly humbles himself and embraces the role of a slave; he willingly accepts humiliation, suffering and even the possibility of death (1:15-21).

Timothy and Ephaphroditus

Although Paul spends only a few verses discussing each of Timothy and Epaphroditus, we can nevertheless see how both of them follow a similar cruciform pattern. Timothy is selfless in his concern for others, thinking not of himself, but only of Christ (2:20-21). Park suggests that we can discern elements of selflessness, servanthood and humility in this brief pen-portrait.[36] Furthermore, he serves Paul, suggesting he is an obedient servant of the gospel (2:22). We can thus detect hints in Timothy of the same cruciform pattern identified in both Jesus and Paul.

A similar argument can be made for Epaphroditus. His selflessness is seen in his concern for the Philippians, even when he is ill (2:26). Paul suggests that this illness is not simply an unfortunate mishap, but is indicative of Epaphroditus' willingness to sacrifice his life for the sake of the gospel and service to the Philippians (2:30).

> Selflessness, which holds the concern of the gospel and others exemplified by servanthood, obedience, humility and willingness to risk his own life, characterizes Epahroditus' actions as those of submission which is consistent with Christ's and Paul's submission.[37]

Cruciform Imitation

We have seen in the argument above the five elements of a cruciform ethic, practised perfectly by Christ and then imitated by Paul, Timothy and Epaphroditus, and commended to the Philippians.[38] They are to submit to the

---

36 Park, *Submission within the Godhead and the Church in the Epistle to the Philippians*, page 128.

37 Park, *Submission within the Godhead and the Church in the Epistle to the Philippians*, page 128.

38 What follows is a summary of Park, *Submission within the Godhead and the Church in the Epistle to the Philippians*, page 129.

call of God on their lives. This submission is characterised by a refusal to exploit rights, privileges and status, which are to be relinquished. This relinquishment leads to embracing servanthood, becoming a slave of God. Those who have taken on the role of a slave voluntarily accept the humiliation and suffering that comes with their station. Christ, Paul and Ephaphroditus all demonstrate how ultimately this must lead to a willingness to embrace death. Finally, all the elements of submission are characterised by selflessness. The cruciform ethic commended by Paul for imitation has at its heart the primacy of others and the possibility of risk to the self. This is a vision of a life lived in glorious weakness.

Imitation should be intelligent

When Paul commends both Christ and himself (and to an extent Timothy and Ephaphroditus) as models for the Philippians to emulate, he in no way advocates a slavish imitation. As Jensen notes in commenting on Philippians 2:1-11, the Philippians are not merely to mimic Christ's actions mindlessly, but rather they are to have the same attitude, as they thoughtfully apply the same virtues that Christ himself displayed.[39]

For this to happen, the Philippians need to know Christ better. In Philippians 3:8, 10, Paul states his desire to *know* Christ. This does not signal simply intellectual or theoretical knowledge about Christ, but rather relational knowledge, obedience to the revelation of God in Christ.

39   Jensen, 'Imitating Paul, imitating Christ', page 21.

Glorious Weakness

We suggest that knowledge of God has two constitutive elements: receipt of revelation of God and then obedience to that revelation, establishing a right relationship with God.[40] This is developed in Phil 3. The idea of receiving revelation from God is implicit in 3:7. Furthermore, Paul shows he has been obedient to that revelation by renouncing his status and the privileges in order to accept the righteousness that comes from God, and so enter into right relationship with him. Fundamentally, the revelation from God is of human sinfulness and need of salvation. Thus the revelation of God comes primarily in the cross and resurrection. Note that when Paul refers to these two (3:10-11), he does so in reverse order, as

> 'Christ's resurrection is proof of God's approval that indeed, the believers' fellowship or salvation, wrought by suffering, is the one that God as approved. Without resurrection, Christ's suffering has no normative status for the believers, and more importantly, no soteriological effect. Knowing Christ in this manner leads to Paul's intentional conformity to Christ's death.'[41]

Knowledge of God is not simply theory. We do have to have an intellectual understanding of our need for Christ, but must more than that, we need to respond with faith and obedience; the knowledge of who God is and what he has done for us shapes how we behave in obedient response.

---

40   Developed from Park, *Submission within the Godhead and the Church in the Epistle to the Philippians*, page 70.
41   Park, *Submission within the Godhead and the Church in the Epistle to the Philippians*, page 74.

Putting it all together: Paul's instructions on giving

Thus far I have identified three elements to Paul's instructions regarding imitation. First, there is a chain of imitation, and in particular Paul presents himself as a paradigm to copy. Second imitation should follow a cruciform pattern, and third, it should be intelligent, applying this pattern to the present situation. Paul's discussion of giving in 2 Corinthians 8 provides a helpful example for how these principles operate.

Paul begins by commending the example of the Macedonian churches to the Corinthian Christians. He then gets to the heart of his theology of giving with this statement: 'For you know the grace of our Lord Jesus Christ, that though he was rich, yet for your sakes he became poor, so that you through his poverty might become rich' (2 Cor. 8:9). Paul freely mixes the association between physical and spiritual riches. Christ was spiritually rich, but became spiritually poor, so that through that the Corinthians who have faith in Christ have spiritual wealth. This spiritual wealth also allows them to recognise the extent of their physical wealth, and so should, as it did in the case of the Macedonians, overflow into material generosity.

We can see how each principle has been put into operation. In this case the chain of imitation is from the Macedonian to the Corinthian church. Paul is not directly involved here, but of course it was he who presented the Macedonian church in Philippi with a clear example of what it means to imitate Christ. Second, we can see how the imitation must be cruciform, as it is the death of Christ which was the means by which the Christians have become spiritually rich. Third, both the Macedonian and then the Corinthian Christians have to think carefully about how to imitate Christ in their present situation. Jesus' death and subsequent resurrection do not directly teach anything about material or financial generosity. But Paul extrapolates the underlying principle of surrender of rights for the benefit of others to a surrender of the right to retain one's possessions in order that others might benefit from them. In this way we can see how he encourages intelligent imitation as the believers model Christ to each other and the world.

Glorious Weakness in our Lives

In one of his letters Luther writes:

'If you are a preacher of mercy, do not preach an imaginary but the true mercy. If the mercy is true, you must therefore bear the true, not an imaginary sin. God does not save those who are only imaginary sinners. Be a sinner, and let your sins be strong, but let your trust in Christ be stronger, and rejoice in Christ who is the victor over sin, death and the world. We will commit sins while we are here, for this life is not a place where justice resides. We, however, says Peter (2 Peter 3:13) are looking forward to a new heaven and a new earth where justice will reign. It suffices that through God's glory we have recognized the Lamb who takes away the sin of the world. No sin can separate us from Him, even if we were to kill or commit adultery thousands of times each day. Do you think such an exalted Lamb paid merely a small price with a meagre sacrifice for our sins? Pray hard for you are quite a sinner.'[42]

42   Section 13 of Letter 99, 1 August 1521 'Let your Sins be Strong: A Letter From Luther to Melanchthon' Translated by Erika Bullmann Flores for Project Wittenberg. Accessed at http://www.iclnet.org/pub/resources/text/wittenberg/luther/letsinsbe.txt on 5th September 2010.

Glorious Weakness

This summarises well the point that I have been making throughout this book: that we are all weak failures and through our weakness we can display God's glory to the world. God has chosen to display his glory through humility which could be understood as weakness. He is not triumphalist or overbearing, he does not force us to worship him or acknowledge him, but rather leaves us free to choose. The weakness of choice, of an offer of love, is that such an offer can be refused or spurned. But the glory of it is that when it is accepted and lived out, it is truly glorious, truly a response of the heart in love and worship.

We are called to live in the same way when we share Christ: not to boast or be triumphalist or forceful, but in humility and weakness to simply present Christ crucified and the redemption of sins that he won for each of us. We must be realists in what we teach and preach. We do not soften the blow of either sin or redemption. We paint a true picture of human depravity, of the fact that we have ignored God and turned our backs on him. But we are also clear as to the extent of God's mercy, of his generosity to sinners who have chosen to ignore him.

This is what Luther means by true mercy and true sin. And when he says we must let our sins be strong, he is not saying we much choose to sin, or that we should put as much effort as possible into sinning. Rather he is telling us to be realists, to recognise that we are all sinners and failures; to not cover up this reality, to not pretend that anything we do is pure or holy or worthy of our God, as everything we do is touched and tainted by sin. Even our best, most noble efforts to serve God and care for others bear the stain and corruption of sin; and so we let our sins be strong. But we let our trust in Christ be stronger, we recognise that although we are stained by sin, his death and resurrection will wash us clean, whiter that the whitest snow, whiter and purer that we could ever dare to imagine. Christ has defeated sin, death and the world, and if we reside in him, then we too can share in that victory.

So now we live a life of weakness, and the glory of God shines through us. But we look ahead to the future glory, the eternal perfection of the world, where every bad thing is removed, and we will bask in the glory of God as we worship and serve him for all eternity in creation made perfect for all who trust in Christ to enjoy. Once we firmly and wholeheartedly put our trust in him we have passed over from death to life, and there is no way we can ever pass back. Even though we will still sin, we are saved and redeemed people, working out our salvation with fear and trembling. Luther comments that we might kill or commit adultery thousands of times a day – given that Jesus tells us even our thought life is sinful, this is far more possible than we might initially want to admit. But even though we are such terrible sinners, it is not enough to separate us from the love of God in Christ Jesus our Lord; and so we can let our sins be strong, but our trust in Christ be all the stronger. The death, resurrection and ascension of Jesus have done all that is needed to win our salvation; the perfect price has been paid. So let Christ's glory shine through your weakness, and may his glory be made known throughout all the world!

Blain Hogan's reflection on 'The Story'[43]

This reflection sums up the point of what I've been trying to say pretty well; read it slowly, and think about what you're going to do...

What will you tell them?

What story will you tell the world?

The one where you win?

Or the one where you lost it all?

Will you show them your beauty and your glory and your fancy clothes?

Or will you show them the mud and dirt that stains the outside of your sleeve?

Will you tell of your hopes and your dreams and the goodness you have seen?

Or will you tell them of the darkness you've created with your own hands?

If you do not tell them both

If you don't tell them the whole story

If you don't tell them all that you have seen

They will never believe you

Now what about what you haven't seen?

Will you tell them of the angels / those messengers of the Lord?

Will you tell them of the invisible kingdom?

Will you tell them of the unseen God?

Will you tell them of the unseen beauty inside their own neighborhoods?

43   Taken from www.blainehogan.com on 2nd October 2010. The item was 'Story 2010 Opener', posted on 27th September 2010.

The unseen beauty inside their own hearts?

The unseen beauty waiting to explode from their broken places?

Listen to me

A New Creation has occurred and we are all asked to participate in it

It / is / unseen

So don't compare your religion and their religion, your rites and their rites, your prophets and their prophets

All this is of no avail

We only want for you to tell them all that you have seen and all that you have not

Tell them that here and there in the world

And now and then in ourselves

Is a New Creation

For the kingdom is now and not yet

Make them feel what you have felt

Sing for them what you have heard

Tell them everything you have and have not seen

For the kingdom is now and not yet

For the kingdom is seen and unseen

Here and there in the world

And now and then in ourselves

Is a New Creation

For the kingdom is now and not yet

For the kingdom is seen and unseen

And you must tell them all about it

This is the Story

Glorious Weakness

Bibliography

Barr, D. D. 'John's Ironic Empire,' *Interpretation* 63 (2009), 20-30.

Black, D. A. *Paul, Apostle of Weakness: Astheneia and Its Cognates in the Pauline Literature* (New York: Peter D Lang, 1984).

Carter, W. 'Matthew's Gospel: An Anti-Imperial/Imperial Reading,' *Currents in Theology and Mission* 34 (2007), 424-33.

Dodd, B. J. *Paul's paradigmatic 'I': personal example as literary strategy* (Sheffield: Sheffield Academic Press, 1999).

Ehrensperger, K. *Paul and the dynamics of power: communication and interaction in the early Christ-movement* (London: T & T Clark, 2007).

Green, J. *New International Commentary on the New Testament: The Gospel of Luke* (Grand Rapids: Eerdmans, 1997).

Hamilton, J. 'The Glory of God in Salvation Through Judgement: The Centre of Biblical Theology?,' *Tyndale Bulletin* 57 (2006), 57-84.

Hays, R. B. 'Embodying the Gospel in Community,' *Menonite Quarterly Review* 74 (2000), 577-85.

Horrell, D. *Solidarity and difference: a contemporary reading of Paul's ethics* (London: T & T Clark, 2005).

Howell, J. R. 'The imperial authority and benefaction of centurions of Acts 10.34-43: a response to C. Kavin Rowe,' *Journal for the Study of the New Testament* 31 (2008), 25-51.

Jensen, M. 'Imitating Paul, imitating Christ: how does imitation work as a moral concept?,' *Churchman* 124 (2010), 17-36.

Lewis, P. *The Message of the Living God* (Leicester: IVP, 2000).

Martin, T. W. 'What Makes Glory Glorious? Reading Luke's Account of the Transfiguration Over Against Triumphalism,' *Journal for the Study of the New Testament* 29 (2006), 3-26.

Park, M. S. *Submission within the Godhead and the Church in the Epistle to the Philippians: An Exegetical and Theological Examination of the Concept of Submission in Philippians 2 and 3.* (London: T & T Clark, 2007).

Wenham, D. *Paul: Follower of Jesus or Founder of Christianity?* (Grand Rapids: Eerdmans, 1995).

Witherington, B. *Conflict and Community in Corinth: A Socio-Rhetorical Commentary on 1 and 2 Corinthians* (Grand Rapids: Eerdmans, 1995).

Lightning Source UK Ltd.
Milton Keynes UK
27 October 2010

161993UK00001B/33/P